THE WILE BIG DERRY PHRASEBOOK

Seamus McConnell

GUILDHALL PRESS

And now there's even more!

THE WILE BIG DERRY PHRASEBOOK

MILLENNIUM CASH-IN EDITION

Compiled by Seamus McConnell

© Guildhall Press 1999
First published November 1996
Reprinted July 1997
This edition October 1999

ISBN 0 946451 55 9

Back cover photographs: Hugh Gallagher
Cover design: GM Photos
Printed by Colour Books, Dublin

GUILDHALL PRESS is an imprint of
GP Media
Unit 4, Community Service Units
Bligh's Lane, Derry BT48 0LZ
T: (02871) 364413
F: (02871) 372949
E: info@ghpress.freeserve.co.uk
W: www.ghpress.freeserve.co.uk

GP Media/Guildhall Press receives financial support from the
District Partnership for the Derry City Council Area under the
European Special Support Programme for Peace and Reconciliation
and from the Londonderry Development Office under the
Londonderry Regeneration Initiative. We would also like to thank
Derry City Council's Recreation and Leisure Department for
generous Community Services Grant Aid.

Foreword

About 1981, because of my general interest in the history of Derry and its people, I got the idea to jot down some of the very humorous sayings unique to our city. As time went on, I began to take seriously the idea of compiling some sort of 'dictionary' of Derry words and phrases, with the vague hope of having it published some day. So around 1984 I got down to some serious research i.e. eavesdropping on peoples conversations, skulking around crowded places like supermarkets and football matches, notebook at the ready, picking up phrases here and there (wakes turned out to be a rich source of material). **Talk of the Town**, first published in 1989, was the end result of all that nosing around.

For a while I believed that I had published the cream of local expressions, but I kept hearing more and more. One day I was sitting in a local cafe and I couldn't help but overhear two ladies 'discussing' a neighbour's little boy and because it sounded so funny I decided there and then that a second book was a must. So **The Folly Up** was published in November 1990.

That had to be it, I thought at the time. But there was still so much out there, I couldn't help writing it all down. Collecting local patois had become almost an obsession. Every time I left the house I found myself seeking out more. I wanted to produce a definitive 'Derry Dictionary'. And then came **The Wile Big Derry Phrasebook**, the complete collection of Derry's very own words, phrases and linguistic peculiarities (except, of course for those I held back for this, the special millennium edition).

Finally, I would like to thank all my family and friends, especially my wife Maeve, for their help and endless patience during the years I have spent working on this series of books. I would also like to thank Paul Hippsley, Adrian Kerr, Joe McAllister, and all the staff of Guildhall Press over the years, who toiled long and hard to put my work into some sort of presentable form, and the local media for the invaluable publicity they have given the books over the years. But most of all I would like to thank the people of Derry who were, unintentionally, the main contributors to this book. I hope that they enjoy reading it as much as I enjoyed writing it.

Seamus McConnell

Millennium Acknowledgements

Guildhall Press would like to thank the last one thousand years, without whose forbearance, and dedication to the cause of coming one after another, in strict numerical order, and without once flinching from that arduous task or bemoaning their station, there would not have been a millennium to cash in on (or learn how to spell). In respect of this, Guildhall Press freely admits, where others deny, that this publication is a blatant attempt to cash in on what is basically just another new year. Calendar and diary manufacturers have, after all, been getting away with it for years now.

We would also like to acknowledge how much this city and its somewhat unique language has changed over the past one thousand years. For instance, one thousand years ago 999 was on the front cover of your diary, not a number you phone in an emergency; English wasn't the major language spoken in Derry, although judging by the contents of this book it still isn't, hi; there were no Derry's Walls, although there may well have been walls in Derry (useful for holding up roofs, painting murals on etc.); Gerry Anderson wasn't on the radio (it only seems like a thousand years) and books hadn't been invented, so this is definitely the first millennium phrasebook.

So, read on, learn and enjoy. By the time the next millennium comes around this book will probably be 'as thick as a docker's wallet' as Seamus keeps discovering new delights of Derry diction.

Contents

MILLENNIUM
EXTRAS

As we move inexorably on towards the new millennium, it becomes increasingly surprising how we managed to survive this one. Modern day fads about healthy eating and exercise seem to be a relatively new thing in Derry, as a quick glance back at old eating habits and (resulting?) illnesses will show. Below is a short menu, a veritable vegetarian's nightmare, of some of the local artery blockers from a few, and not so few, years ago. It's surprising there are any pigs left in Derry at all.

The Derry Diet

Bacon Ends
General bits and pieces left over from the pig when all the good bits have been removed.

Black/White Puddin'
The main ingredient of this delicacy is blood, either cows' or pigs', with a few other dubious extras thrown in for good measure. A must for any self-respecting fry-up.

Chain Bones
From the spine of the pig (again), very popular in the preparation of soups and stews, but considered very tasty when cooked on their own.

Forced Meat
More commonly known as 'mince' but so called because slabs of meat were forced in one end of a machine and the mince emerged from the other.

Hocks
Cuts from the shank or rear end of the ubiquitous pig, usually eaten with ubiquitous chips.

Knobs/Pigs' Feet
A beautiful culinary delight when cooked with cabbage and spuds and much sought after by food experts in bygone days. In victualler's terms, the knobs were the knuckles from the pig's feet, because pigs don't have hands, apparently.

Necks

As the name suggests, these were the neck and upper part of the pig's anatomy used in the preparation of various dishes and evidently very tasty.

Rissoles

Round flat bits of meat covered in what looked like sawdust, and made from an array of indeterminate ingredients.

Shins

The front part of the cow's leg and, apparently, flush with mouth-watering meat.

Skirts

Nothing to do with ladies' clothing, but actually the inside of a pig's ribcage. They adorned manys a table on a Sunday in the forties and fifties, when, no pun intended, times were a bit on the lean side.

Special Mince

No longer known by this name, but called 'hamburger meat'. James Doherty was the most famous manufacturer of this delicacy and a plentiful supply of a similar meat can still be found today.

Tripe

The contents of a cow's stomach much sought after in the 'good old days' but not eaten a lot today.

Tails

No explanation needed here, so I'll explain. These could be either cows' or pigs' tails which were widely eaten years ago. I don't know how they tasted, but they must have looked strange sticking out of the pot and adorning the plate.

Strange Ailments Prevalent in the Derry Area

Bile
Large pimple type thing which can appear on any part of the body. Not life threatening but very painful. Just one sure cure known to man and that's to stick the neck of a glass bottle filled with boiling water on to the head of it, which can't be taken off until it's been completely drawn out. Although this can cause great distress to the patient, it's always great watching it being done to some poor cratur.

Futrot
In the forties and fifties it was noticed that a lot of children were coming home from school complaining of 'wrinkly' feet. Their parents also noticed that their children's feet were very smelly and a deathly white colour. At first doctors were sceptical about the problem but then they had to admit that the condition did exist. Although extensive research was carried out, the best medical minds of the time couldn't determine the cause of the condition. They also noticed that in some cases these symptoms were accompanied by a painful red ring around the upper calf part of the leg. It was quite by accident that the truth of the matter was finally established when Wabbits McClean, out riding his brakeless bicycle, fell off and twisted his ankle. At the hospital the doctors struggled to get his boots off, and when they finally did, they discovered he was in an advanced state of futrot. It was then that it finally struck them and they discovered the cause of this chronic complaint... ill fitting waterboots that were letting in!

Light Head
This condition causes the patient to stagger and stumble about all over the place, and generally make a nuisance of himself. For a long time the cause was unknown, but then they realised that it was brought on by too much air getting in through the ears. After discovering that, the cure was simple: wear ear muffs.

The Jandies
Moderately serious condition caused by malfunction of the liver, and brought on by certain other medical conditions. Can also be triggered by the disgusting behaviour of some individuals, like blowing their nose onto the street, hence the expression, 'You give me the jandies'. (Symptoms may include a yellowing of the skin.)

Bokeys
The dread of all parents! Living creatures stomping around in their child's hair with impunity. This condition is contracted when one child who is infected

comes into close contact with other children. Close contact can mean anything within a half mile as these 'bokeys' haver been known to jump at least five hundred yards. Some can grow up to a foot in length and if not tackled quickly they have been know to make a rope from the child's hair, especially if it's long, and drag them down to the quay. The most effective way to get rid of them is to shave the child completely bald and rub a mixture of Jeyes Fluid and H.P. sauce into the scalp three times a day and once more at bed time.

Waterbrash

This is a digestive disorder where the sufferer is plagued by constant bouts of heartburn accompanied by the spewing up of an acid filled clear fluid. The sufferer usually spits the foul tasting liquid into the fire which causes a massive flame to flare up and at times was such that it kept the house warm all night. The most severe case was reported to be a man from the Creggan Heights area who is said to have brought up the biggest waterbrash on record, although it's not officially recognised by the Guinness Book of Records. Apparently it was around a gallon and a half.

The Skitters

A looseness of the bowels necessitating swift and frequent sojurns to the loo. Probably caused by the consumption of too many fries or curries. Can be most alarming for the sufferer and the general public alike if an attack occurs in the city centre where toilets are few and far between. They say that eating an Oxo cube helps. It doesn't actually cure it, but can thicken it up a bit. Alternatively, bicycle clips can be worn.

Brongkitis

Used to be a very serious disease in times gone by but not too bad these days. It affects the lungs causing inflammation with bouts of coughing and wheezing. Probable cause is sitting in too many bingo halls and pubs inhaling the smoke from too many fags. In the past, removal of one or both lungs was the only cure, but nowadays it's just a matter of spending your leisure time in the smoke-free environment of the Bru.

The Gimmies

This disease is found mainly in children, but can affect adults as well. The strange thing about it is that it can cause greater pain to the people around the patient than the patient himself. The main symptoms to watch for are the incessant nerve racking demands of the patient crying, 'gimmie this' or 'gimmie that', and the inevitable huffing in the corner if he/she doesn't get what he/she wants. If left unchecked the child could be murdered. There's only one tried and tested cure, and that's to swathe the child's head in plaster of paris and feed him/her intravenously.

The Pip
A disconcerting mental disorder instigated by the childish and infuriating behaviour of people with whom the sufferer just happens to disagree. It spurs the patient to assail the offending individual with a tirade of abuse by hurling uncomplimentary statements such as 'You sicken my happiness' or 'You're a mouth so ye are' at the person concerned. In most cases the condition is only temporary, but unfortunately in some it can be permanent; my advice is to stay well clear of anyone afflicted by this nasty illness. A cure can be effected by just being very nice to the patient.

Wanderin' Han' Syndrome (W.H.S)
This illness is mainly confined to the male of the species, although it's reported that on rare occasions females can suffer from it too. The first person to notice the symptoms is usually the patient's girlfriend when she suspects that her boyfriend's hand is beginning to move tentatively towards forbidden areas of her person. If nipped in the bud by the lady administering a good slap in the bake to the offender, there usually will be no more problems. If, however, due to the lady's unwillingness to cause embarassment, or worse, get dumped, the condition is allowed to get out of control, and once the offending limb reaches a certain area, I'm afraid the disease has become incurable.

Wakeness
A sudden feeling of being unwell with symptoms like dizziness and shaking. It can be physical or brought on by an attack of nerves. If confronted by someone who's having an attack do not tell them to 'Wise up' or 'Get a grip wud ye' or you'll only make matters worse. The best thing to do is to take them to the nearest pub and fill them full of brandy. This should calm them down a bit and alleviate the symptoms. If this doesn't work threaten to tell the Electricity Board that they're fiddling the meter. This should do the trick.

Gammy Leg
This disease seems to be endemic to professional footballers, and particularly to ones in the Brandywell area. In the majority of cases it only affects one leg, but it can strike at both and when it does the results can be disastrous. Diagnosis of the condition can be tricky, but the general medical consensus seems to indicate that anyone suffering from the disorder appears to display an inordinate inability to run or kick a ball. It also seems to impair their sense of direction, making it almost impossible for players, especially the front runners, to find the goalposts. Various cures, such as frequent sacking of managers, resignations of directors and so on have been tried, but apparently with little or no success. A new treatment has recently been tried, but that too seems to have failed. It involves bringing in players from all arts and parts, like Ballybofey, Omagh or Nigeria, letting them play for a week or so, and then packing them off back home again. This extreme remedy has also failed miserably to halt the insidious progression of the disease. The only possible answer seems to be prevention, and that means a thorough scan on the

G.O.A.L. (Gamminess of a Leg) detector machine, and hopefully the disease will be identified early enough for it to be treated successfully.

Mad Cab Disease (M.C.D.)

This is a serious disorder that seems to turn the sufferers into deranged monsters. The disease is confined almost exclusively to taxi drivers, and it has almost reached epidemic proportions. The first symptoms are a tendency to cause traffic jams and block whole streets, especially Sackville Street and William Street, with 15 year-old Nissan Bluebirds or brand new Vauxhall Cavaliers. As the disease progresses, far more serious symptoms may manifest themselves, such as an irresistible urge to blare horns in the middle of the night and a complete mental blindness to the existence of other road users. In extreme cases more deadly signs, like driving along footpaths and driving out of side streets without stopping, may appear.

Wile Dose a Coul

This is a relatively minor ailment but can have an assortment of unpleasant symptoms such as a snottery nose, and germ laden bouts of sneezing and coughing. In extreme cases, when the patient complains of 'feelin' cat' or 'wake as watter', other symptoms may appear such as 'slabbers'. Unfortunately there is no known cure, but sometimes taping a jar of Vick to the sufferer's nose helps alleviate the symptoms.

Tillophobia

This is one of those little understood mental disorders that only seems to afflict certain sections of the population, in this instance, supermarket checkout girls. The symptoms aren't difficult to recognise. The first indication that something is wrong is whenever shoppers waiting in the queue suddenly engage in protracted sighing and shuffling of feet as the girl at the checkout seems to have downed tools in order to discuss the previous night's crack at the disco with her colleague at the adjacent till. This phase can sometimes be curtailed by one of the shoppers threatening to call the manager, 'If she dosen't shut her bake'. The second stage of the illness may then set in, with the checkout girl's face assuming a strange vacant expression, as all the people in the queue collectively receive a telepathic message from the victim which says, 'I hate this job so I'm goin' ti' mik youse suffer, so I am'. This stage in the illness is usually followed by the patient abruptly disappearing from the scene altogether, to return five minutes later when the agitation in the queue has turned to open hostility with lots of cursing and swearing. In the final stages of this disorder the checkout lady may suddenly declare to the eriously exhausted shoppers standing in the queue with their bulging trollies: 'This desk is now closed, move on down please'. She then pulls a chain across the passageway and stomps off, causing a near riot as trollies, baskets and shoppers scramble to the nearest, shortest queue, where, inevitably, 'the till roll has just run out...'

Who Wants To Be A Millenniumaire?

1 By what name was the city first known?
A Doire Colmcille
B Doire Calgach
C Londondoire Calgach
D Thon hill over there, beside that big river

2 Which Saint wrote the first biography of Colmcille?
A St Bernard
B St Andgreavsie
C St Adamnan
D St Johnstone

3 Which King laid siege to Derry in 1688?
A King James I
B King William
C King James II
D King Edward potato

4 Which gate did the Apprentice Boys shut in 1688?
A Shipquay Gate
B The garden gate
C Ferryquay Gate
D Watergate

5 Who, or what, does the skeleton on the city's coat of arms represent?
A Chris DeBurgh
B Halloween
C Sir Walter DeBurgo
D A big dog's dinner

6 Where was Derry's first town hall built?
A Guildhall Square
B Derry
C The Diamond
D In a factory

7 What does the city's motto 'Vita Veritas Victoria' mean?
A Not much
B Life, Truth, Victory
C Life, Liberty and Fruit of the Loom
D Hurry up, Victoria, taxi's waiting

8 Where was Derry's first gas-works?
A Guildhall Council Chamber
B Brandywell
C Public toilets in Waterloo Place
D Bridgend ('cause it was cheaper there)

9 What did the initials BSR stand for?
A Big Shiny Records
B Birmingham Sound Reproducers
C Binlids, Stone throwers and Riots
D Bogside Scouts' Regiment

10 What was the name of Dana's Eurovision winner?
A The Town I Loved So Well
B All Kinds Of Everything
C. A Whole Handlin'
D Teenage Kicks

Answers on a postcard please. Winners will receive a free copy of the next Millennium Wile Big Derry Phrasebook, and loads more besides. Closing date for entries is 12 noon, 31/12/2999. No entries will be accepted after the closing date. So, call a mucker, go evens or ask the regulars, but don't forget, final answers only please.

THE TEN COMMANDMENTS – DERRY STYLE

1st – Thou shalt call the city by its true name, either Derry or Londonderry, not that most derisive of terms 'Stroke City'.

2nd – Thou shalt support thy team each Sabbath day at the Brandy by shouting abuse at the man dressed in black.

3rd – Thou shalt not get caught working and drawing the Bru.

4th – Thou shalt not tap off yer Ma (except on Friday nights for a few swallys).

5th – Thou shalt not covet thy neighbour's greyhound, pigeon, or new satellite dish.

6th – Thou shalt not wait in the car reading the Tilly outside the supermarket while the wife does the shopping.

7th – Thou shalt eat two baps a day, minimum.

8th – Thou shalt not drive in Waterloo Place (unless you feel like it).

9th – Thou shalt besport thyself in white socks and a 'tache.

10th – Thou shalt walk thy greyhound twice a day (except when it's raining).

11th – Thou shalt learn to work out to the nearest wing a 50p reverse forecast yankee.

OVERHEARD CONVERSATIONS

1st Lady: De ye see if I had thon boy, ah'd draw the back a may han' across ay's ja'bone.

2nd Lady: Aye ah know wat ye mean. God ay's wile disabeejint. Wan word from ay's moller an ay diz wat ay liks.

1st Lady: Lay oller day ay putt in ma wunda ye know. See if I hadda catched 'im, ah'd a busted ay's snotter, so ah wudd. God ah wuz ragin' so ah wuz.

2nd Lady: Ah doh know wat the young wans're comin' ti these days. When I wuz a wane we'd a wee bitta thought fur wur nibbers, so way had.

1st Lady: Ah well, the sooner we git a shift from thon pliss the better. C'mon we'd better git the rest a wur messages before the town gits black.

1st Lady: De ye know sumpfin Surra? Lay oller day my Shooey wuz tikkin' in wi' ay's leg.

2nd Lady: Och God Murry, am wile sarry ti' hear that. Wat happened ti' 'im?

1st Lady: Well wan night ay sid ay wuz gittin' a bit of a dose, so ay went upstairs ti' throw 'imself down, but on ay's way up ay slipped an' twusted ay's knee. Ay wuz roarin' outta 'im wi' pain so we haddy phone the amblins an' hiv 'im shifted ti' Altygalvin immejitly. Ah felt a wile pity fur 'im an' ah hivn't an eye in may head since so ah hivn't.

2nd Lady: Och don't wurry. Sure it wuz the same wi' may moller when she fell an' horted 'er hench, but she wuz dead on a wik lidder.

1st Lady: Am g'in ore the night ti' see 'im so am are, wanny come wi' may?

2nd Lady: Naw ah canny gore the night Murry, but al bibbildy gore the marra evenin'.

1st Lady: Okey doke Surra, ah might run in ti' ye over there, orr ite?

2nd Lady: Orr ite Murry, see ye after.

CONFUSED? WELL READ ON...

Catch Yursel' On

THE wile BIG DERRY PHRASEBOOK

PART 1

TALK OF THE TOWN

A Big Wane: An immature person.

Acks: Ask.

A 'Clare Tay Me Clogs: O dearie me!

Actin' The Cod: Pretending; fooling around.

Act Lik A Christian: Conform to accepted standards of behaviour.

Affected: Not in control of all one's faculties.

Affronted: Acutely embarrassed.

A Fis Fur Ivry Day A The Week An' Two Fur A Sunday: Untrustworthy.

Agger: Argue.

A Good Booter/Steever: A hard kick administered to another individual.

Ah Canny: I cannot.

Aikey: Awkward.

All Away Wi' Yursel': Proud; happy.

All Biz: Going about one's activities enthusiastically.

All Broke: Sheepishly embarrassed.

A Lock A Hippince: Small amount of money.

Am Are So: I am indeed.

Am Sure You're Unazy: You're not worried at all.

Am Tellin' On Ye: Child's threat to inform parents of another child's misdeed or displeasing actions.

An' All: Etcetera; and so on.

Annie No Rattle: One who pipes up at the end of a conversation.

Any Danger Ay A Start? Question by person not over-enthusiastic about commencing employment.

Are Ye Rightly? I hope you're well.

Are Ye Sick? You must be joking!

Are Ye Talking Ti' Me Or Blowin' Yur Nose/Chewin' A Breek? Said in anger when someone doesn't like the tone of another's voice.

A' Right Hi? How are you?

As Big A Liar As John Green: Description of someone disinclined to tell the truth; a teller of tall tales.

Ashy Pet: One who seldom leaves the house or who hugs the fireplace.

As Much: A lot.

As Nice As Ninepince: Phoney friendliness; insincere behaviour.

Ast: Requested.

A Trick Above Yur Capers: Telling someone not to push their luck.

A Waitin' On: Dying.

Awantin': Message issued when a child's immediate presence is required by its parents.

Away Wi' The Donkey: Lost, whereabouts unknown.

A Wee Hoult: An embrace with a girl or boy.

A Wee Outin's: Short trip to the seaside etc.

A Wee Priest: Description of any young priest, regardless of size.

A Wee Scoot Over: A quick visit.

A Whole Bang Jang: An abundance of.

A Whole Hanlin': A confused and complicated situation.

A Whole Rake: A large amount of anything, exact quantity unknown.

Aw, What Are Ye Talkin' About? Say no more as you're talking nonsense.

Aye: Yes.

Aye Surely: Of course!

A Zed: Sarcastic answer to the question "why?"

Backwater: What a person hasn't got when they speak their mind.

Badly Bent: Almost embarrassed.

Badly Stuck: Insufficient funds to carry out plans.

Bad Swally: Fast eater.

Bags: Lots of.

Bake: Face or mouth.

Bang On: Just right; ideal; great.

Banty: Bow legged.

Bargin' A Bucketful: Expressing grave displeasure.

Bars: News; gossip; boyfriend or girlfriend.

Bat In The Mouth: A thump or punch in the face.

Batter On: Continue on ahead.

Bealin': Festering or inflamed wound.

Beaten Docket: One with all resources exhausted; a situation beyond reprieve.

Beaten Rotten: Completely overwhelmed; totally defeated.

Beat 'Im At The Boots: Game devised by parents to fool kids into getting undressed for bed.

Better: Having given birth.

Big An' Ugly Enough: Well able; capable of acting on one's own initiative.

Big Lump: Large child; ungainly person.

Big Man: One who threatens; a bully.

Big Night: Party or celebration.

Bile: Boil (like a pimple).

Binder: A person guilty of rash and illogical behaviour; an idiot.

Bird Mouthed: Reluctant to speak up or complain.

Bite The Nose Off: Snap at; argue with.

Blab: Unwelcome swelling on tyre or football.

Blarge: Powerful but unstylish kick of a football.

Blatter: Burst of gunfire.

Bleach: Hit viciously.

Bleezin': Burning vigorously.

Blew Out: Rebuffed or rejected by the object of one's desires.

Blootered: Excessively inebriated.

Blurt: Disparaging name for someone not well liked.

Bockle: Child's term for a common glass container.

Boggin': Very dirty; x-rated (of films).

Bog Yur Arm In: Take advantage of; make the best of.

Bokey: Nit or other insect in scalp.

Boller: Trouble or aggravation.

Bombed Out: All romantic connections terminated unexpectedly for no apparent reason.

Boney: Large commemorative open-air fire.

Boodles: Glass marbles.

Boul: Container for soup, porridge, etc.

Boul' Brat: Impudent child.

Boulted: Ran away hurriedly.

Boys A Boys: Exclamation of surprise and wonderment.

Brave: Good or fine as in "a brave day"; also emphatic use as in "brave and big".

21

Breek: Lump of stone.

Broke Dead: Insulted, ignored or extremely embarrassed.

Broke Fur Ye: Sympathetic embarrassment due to the unfortunate circumstances of another.

Broke To The Bone: Very embarrassed.

Bru: Labour exchange; social security office.

Bucketin': Raining heavily.

Buck-Leppin': Jumping about in a frivolous but irksome fashion.

Budgen Hook: Buncrana train.

Bummin' Yur Load: Boasting about one's supposed abilities or achievements.

Burl: Turn or swing round quickly.

Burnie: Very hot, therefore not to be touched.

Buy Now While Shops Last: Sign of the times.

Cacky: Dirty; light admonition to child not to touch.

Cannel: A candle.

Can't Houl Yur Water: Unable to keep a secret; indiscreet.

Can't See Fur Lukin': Staring ignorantly.

Can't Thole: Unable to stand or tolerate

Car On: Go on about your business.

Carryin': Having surplus money on one's person.

Cat: Very bad; disappointing.

Catched: Caught red handed; taken for a ride.

Catch Yursel' On: Come to your senses; don't be silly.

Cat Melojin: Terrible; really bad.

Cat's Fur, Did Ye Iver See It On A Dog? Sarcastic answer to the question "what for?"

Champ: Mixture of bread and tea.

Chancer: Sly person; a conman.

Change Yur Tune: Adopt a different attitude.

Cheesed Off: Fed up.

Cheevy: Chase; run after.

Chimley: That part of the house which allows smoke from the fire to escape.

Chinstrap: Black ring around child's neck caused by failure to wash.

Chip John: Any business man who overcharges.

Cleared: Ran off; disappeared.

Click: To succeed in romance.

C'meer A Wee Minute: To attract someone's attention with a view to telling them something secret or important.

C'meer But Hi: On second thoughts.

C'meer Hi: Would you mind coming over here as I want to talk to you?

Coffin Nails: Old fashioned brands of strong cigarettes.

Contrary: Awkward; obstinate; argumentative.

Cooter: Face.

Corned Beef Tin: Small community centre in Creggan Estate, Derry.

Corns: Currants.

Corp: Derogatory name for a useless person.

Corporation Hair Oil: Tap water used for hair styling when times were hard.

Could Be Heard At Doho: Very loud.

Couldn't Git Over: Amazed; couldn't comprehend the situation.

Coul Rife: One who's always complaining about the cold.

Coul Snotter: Description of someone ignored, abandoned or stood up.

Crabbit: Bad tempered; irritable.

Cran': Machinery for lifting heavy loads.

Cruddles: Curdled milk spat out by babies.

Crummles: Particles of bread.

Crunnion: Head.

Culchie: Anybody who doesn't live in Derry.

Curly Water: Mixture of sugar and water supposed to make hair curl.

Dake: Small sum of money given back to unlucky gambler.

Damnedable: Terrible; awful.

Damned Apt: Appropriate; totally right or fitting.

Dander At Yur Cush: Stroll at your leisure.

Dashin': Raining heavily.

Dead Chip: Not very dear.

Dead If Ye'd The Wit To Stiffen: Not looking too well.

Deadly: Great; to be admired.

Dead Nip: Mysterious black mark appearing overnight on body

Dead On: Just great; giving satisfaction.

Dead On, Dickie Valley: I don't quite believe you.

Death On: Very much opposed to.

Debtor: Creditor.

Ded'ner: A person to be wary of.

Deef: Hard of hearing.

Desprit: Terrible.

Deuce: Two pence in "old" money.

Devalve: Give up; stop talking; be quiet.

23

Dew Points: Large American chemical factory at Maydown.

De Ye? Do you?

Dial: Face.

Dickied Up: Well dressed in preparation for a special event.

Die Wi' That Face An' Nobody'll Wash Ye: Cheer up! Don't be so downhearted or you'll put people off.

Dirty Baste: Immoral or unclean character.

Dirty Butter: Person who seldom washes.

Dirty Luk: Facial expression of disapproval.

Disease: Description of obnoxious person.

Do As You're Bid: Request to obey.

Dobbin': Staying away from school without consent.

Dock Horney: Harbour policeman.

Doesn't Miss A Bar: Knows everything that is going on; a nosey person.

Dogged: Unfair; mean.

Doing The Dog: Causing disappointment; playing a dirty trick on someone.

Donkeys: A long time.

Don't Be There 'Til You're Back: Hurry up.

Don't Kick That Cap, There's A Man Under It: He's a bit on the small side; jovial remark about a person's stature.

Don't Sicken Me Happiness: Don't annoy me; leave me alone.

Don't Stand Sideways Or Ye'll Be Reported Missing: Unkindly remark to thin person.

Don't Tik Him On: Take no notice of him.

Doof: Beat up; assault.

Doorstep: Thick slice of bread.

Dooter: Lag behind; dally aimlessly.

Dootsie: Old fashioned; corny; childish.

Down To Budgen: Up to Buncrana.

Do Ye Think I Came Up The Foyle In A Bubble: I'm not as naive as you may think.

Do Ye Want A Medal? Sarcastic reply to boaster.

Dragged Up: Badly reared by parents.

Drowneded: Completely soaked; drowned.

Dry Up: Forceful request to stop talking.

Dry Yur Eyes: Stop moaning or complaining.

Duckle: A gormless or cowardly person.

Dunt: To thump.

Durr: Entrance to a building.

Dyin' About: Very fond of.

Easy Goin' Tam: A calm individual; not easily ruffled.

Eat The Fis A: Violently take issue with; to scold.

Eejit: One who engages in clownish acts.

Effin' An' Blindin': Swearing profusely.

Ekker: Homework.

Elected: Situation where the required result is likely.

Empy: Not full; to beat someone up.

Enough A That An' More A The Ollor: Jovial resistance to a romantic approach.

Evenin': Afternoon.

Eyed: Caught sight of.

Eye Ye? Are you?

Fading Away Ti' An Elephant: Putting on weight.

Failed: Having lost weight; sick looking.

Fair Chanter: Good singer.

Fair Doos: Good luck to you.

Fairly: Flexible measurement of size, speed, time, etc., as in "fairly moving" or "fairly big".

Fall In Ti' Beef: Put on weight.

Fall In Wi': Meet; join up with.

Far Out As Kit Logue: Wrong; way off the mark.

Far Shuk: Health badly deteriorated; changed for the worse.

Feardy Custard: Easily scared; timid person.

Fernenst: Situated or positioned opposite.

Filums: The moving pictures; movies.

Fire Maygade: Body of men dedicated to extinguishing unwanted fires.

Fis: Face.

Fis As Long As The Day An' The Morra: Down in the dumps; sorry for oneself.

Fis Lik A Busted Boot: Not good looking.

Fis Lik The Back Ay A Bus: Very ugly.

Fisslin': Soft scratching sound; sound of light movement.

Fissy: Light insult.

Flake It: Fall asleep; faint or die.

Flay: Flea.

Fluer: Inner lower surface of a room.

Flume: Polite swear word.

Flyin': Doing well; very successful.

Fly Man: Crafty fellow; one to be watched.

Folly: Tag along behind.

Footerin': Tinkering or messing about; using delaying tactics.

Forbye: As well; also.

Fork: Opening at front of trousers.

Forty Coats: Name given to person who's over-clothed.

Foundered: Very cold.

Fraud The Beetle: A cheat.

Frosty Face: Joker in pack of cards.

Full: Drunk and incapable.

Fur Nothin': Useless; totally without merit.

Fur The Altar: About to receive communion in church.

Futpad: Pavement.

Gab: Country dweller.

Gansey: Pullover; expression of approval.

Geemidy God!: Exclamation of disbelief/exasperation.

Germans: Paris buns.

Gern The Weller: One who moans about the climatic conditions.

Gimme Head Peace: Stop annoying me.

Git A Start: Find employment.

Git Away: You don't say.

Git Away A That Wi' Ye: I don't believe you.

Git In There, Norton: Didn't I do well?

Git Off: Close encounter with the opposite sex, usually at a dance/disco.

Git Off Ye: Get undressed.

Git Ontay: Take issue with or reprimand someone about their actions.

Git On Ye: Get dressed.

Git Shot: Go away; take yourself off.

Gittin' As Big: Growing up.

Git Up Them Stairs (Or I'll Buy A Bungalow): Isn't life wonderful?

Git Yur Foda Tuk: Have your photograph taken.

Git Yur Head Shired: Get away from it all; find peace.

Git Yur Pot Scripped: Go to the confessional box to declare past misdeeds.

Git Yur Rag Up: Muster some courage; get angry.

Giv' Us Share: Give me some.

Glar: Thick oozy mud.

Gleed: Glimmer of light in fire; an idea.

Gleek: Quick look; often sneakily.

Glengorm: Dirt; muck.

Go An' Scratch: Don't bother me; leave me alone.

God Bliss's An' Save's: May the Almighty have pity and protect me.

God Bliss The Mark: Expression of sympathy for one afflicted with illness or disablement.

God Forgive Ye: Reproach for speaking ill of someone; expression of horror at another's irreverence.

God Luk To Yur Wit: You're naive; you haven't much chance of success.

God's Gift: Chauvinist male with delusions of grandeur.

Goin' Spare: At wit's end; cracking under pressure.

Goney: Going to; about to.

Good Steam: Funny; humorous; enjoyable.

Googy: Cross-eyed.

Go On Yur Neck: Stumble or fall.

Goose Gab: Bitter fruit.

Go Round Meg's To You: It's difficult to get you to understand anything; you're basically stupid.

Gover Yur Notes: To lecture someone at length.

Gran': Feeling healthy, fit or well.

Gravy Ring: Doughnut with a hole.

Grazy: Greasy, usually of chips.

Grunter: Incompetent footballer.

Gub: Mouth.

Guilthall: Large ornate building where City Council sits.

Gulderin': Roaring or shouting.

Gunk: A setback or surprise.

Hacker: A footballer whose kicking is not confined to the ball.

Hage: Row of bushes between fields or gardens.

Hair: Fight between females with a view to extracting some hair from opponent.

Half-A-Dollar: 12 ½ new pence; 2s. 6d. in "old" money.

Half-A-Man: Derogatory appraisal of a male.

Hallion: A rough character who behaves coarsely at times.

Hammered: Exhausted; unlucky; heavily defeated.

Hangin' From Me Upper Lip: Sarcastic answer to someone inquiring after another's location.

Hard: Stingy.

Hard As Goats' Knees/Knap Stones: Very tough.

Hard Ticket: Tough character; a good street fighter.

Harley: Hardly; barely. (Nothing to do with motorbikes!).

Hateful Jas: Unlikeable person.

Have A Notion A: Take a fancy to (usually) a girl/boy.

Have A Titter A Wit: Have some sense; behave correctly.

Have I Anything On Me Belongin' Ti' Ye? Sarky comment when a person catches someone else staring at them.

Having All Yur Orders: Pampered; spoiled.

Header: Slightly unbalanced person with a tendency to act illogically.

Headin': Leaving; going off.

Head The Grittins: Aggressive person given to wildly excessive acts.

Heart Lik A Swingin' Breek: Unfeeling; emotionally cold.

**He'd Steal The Eye Out A Yur Head And
(1) Tell Ye Yer Wur Better Lukin' Wi'out It:
(2)Come Back An' Spit In The Hole:**
He's a thief.

Heeds 'N' Thras: All mixed up; bits and pieces.

Heel: Bottom or last slice of bread.

Hench: Hip bone.

Here's Me: This is what I did/said.

**He Wudn't Give Ye
(1)A Scare If He Wuz A Ghost:
(2)A Lift If Ye Wur In A Coffin:**
He's a bit tight with his money.

Hi: Much-used but meaningless ending to most Derry speech. Exclamation with the intent of attracting someone's attention.

Hippins: Nappies.

Hit: It.

Hoachin': Filled with, as in "river hoachin' with fish"; smelly or dirty.

Hock: Forced to carry something (or drag it along) against one's will.

Hocklin': Coughing; trying to clear chest or throat.

Hoke: A blow with the elbow; dig around in search of something.

Holly Eve: Hallowe'en.

Hoosh A Wee Balo: Derry lullaby.

Horted: In pain; injured.

Houl Yur Whisht: Shut up!

How're Ye Fixed, Mucker? Solicitous inquiry about a person's financial status with a view to requesting a temporary loan.

How's It Cuttin'/Goin': Friendly inquisitive greeting.

How's The Form? Are you well?

How Wud Ye Lik Yur Head In Yur Hand? I may have to resort to violence to resolve this problem.

How Ye, Burke? Nothing doing?

Huffy Snotter: Someone who's prone to sulking.

I Believe Ye Where Thousands Wouldn't: I don't believe you.

I Don't Boil Me Cabbage Twice: I don't repeat myself.

I Don't Know Meself The Day: Something good has happened; I feel better than I did yesterday.

If Ye'd All Austins On Ye Ye'd Still Luk The Same: Your dress sense is questionable.

If Ye Don't Lik It Ye Know What Ti Do: Like it or lump it; it's your decision.

I Haven't The Nails To Scratch Meself: I have no money to do anything.

I'll Bust Your Clock: I'll strike you in the face.

I'll Buy Ye A Rattly: Don't be so childish.

I'll Give Ye A Shout: I'll call for you later.

I'll Knock Your Pan In: I'll beat you about the head.

I'll Stick The Nut In Ye: I'll head butt you.

I Luked At Better An' Niver Wuz Checked: Angry riposte to "What are you looking at?"

I'm As Glad: Expression of delight, usually at another's misfortune.

I'm Gaspin' Fur A Reek: I'd love a cigarette.

I'm Oney Keepin' Ye Goin': I'm only jesting with you.

I'm Ready Fur Down The Strand: I'm close to a nervous breakdown.

I'm Sure I Wull: I will not.

I'm Wile Dry: I'm thirsty.

I Nearly Died: I was very embarrased/shocked.

In Ernie: For real; seriously intent upon the matter at hand.

Is The Skin Of Yur Head Tight? What do you take me for?

It'll Turn Ti' A Pig's Fut: Unsympathetic reply to someone who complains of their wounds.

It's A Pity A Ye: It serves you right.

It's Lik A Bottle: The road is very slippery due to snow or ice.

It's No Odds: It doesn't matter.

It's Well Seen: It's very obvious.

It Wud Cut Ye/Skin Ye: It's very cold.

It Wud Fit Ye Better: Another course of action would be more beneficial all round.

It Wud Melt Ye: It's very warm.

Jibblin': Splashing around with water.

Jist: Usual answer to the question "why?" when no justification can be found.

Jist Fur Badness: Weak excuse for something being done in spite of another's objections.

Join: Scold or reprimand.

Jook: A quick look.

Jube On: Become aware of what's happening.

Jumpin': Very angry; upset.

Jute Box: Record-playing machine.

Jack-An-Ory: Scornful statement of disbelief.

Jandies: Jaundice; state of revulsion.

Jawbox: Old style enamel sink.

Keek: Blow with foot.

Keepin' Dick: Acting as look-out during secretive undertaking.

Kilt: Severely reprimanded; killed.

Kip: Establishment of dubious reputation.

Knack A The Mug: Dexterity at playing marbles.

Know What's Stickin' Ti' Ye: Be painfully aware of someone's retribution.

Knyuck: Steal.

Linky Long Legs: Tall thin person.

Landed: In a promising position for further success.

Lashin': Raining heavily.

Latchico: Undesirable character; hanger-on.

Laughin': Doing well; on the path to success.

Least A Me Notion: Last thing on my mind.

Leenge: Make swinging blow at; jump at.

Left Lik A Kiltie: Left standing alone and embarrased.

Leggered: Covered in dirt, muck or other unsightly substances.

Leller: Cowhide.

Lettin' On: Pretending to tell the truth.

Level: Knock someone to the ground.

Lift Yur Feet: Hurry up.

Lik A Rake: Very thin; lightly built.

Lik Nellie Ramsey's: Very untidy (as of house).

Lik Shipquay Gate: Quite large or wide; of gross proportions.

Lik Soups: That's highly improbable.

Lik The Oul Woman's Stews: Unwelcome; disliked.

Lipton's Orphan: Pitiful child.

Livin': Infested with fleas or lice; dirty.

Lock: Indefinable amount of anything.

Lodger: Small uncut loaf of bread.

Long Shootie: Street football game where ball is kicked from "goal" to "goal" with no outfield play.

Long Trams: Tall gangly person.

Loo Warm: Tepid.

Losin' The Bap: Getting angry or annoyed.

Luks More Lik 'Imself Now: Sympathetic comment usually addressed to a corpse at a wake.

Lured: Happy; excited; pleased.

Lured Stiff: Delighted.

Lyin': Confined to bed; ill.

32

Make: Half-penny in "old" money.

Make A Rise: Make some money, usually from gambling.

Make A Tear At: Rush at in anger.

Make A Winde At: Lash out wildly with fist.

Man Dear: Expression of jovial surprise.

Me Han' On Yur ....: I like your.....

Me Head's Deeved: I can't stand it anymore; fed up with something.

Mell: Violently strike.

Me Lone: On my own; by myself.

Mibby: Perhaps.

Mind: Remember.

Mind Ye: Assertion of truth.

Mingin': Dirty and smelly.

Mingy: Not very generous.

Mizzlin': Raining lightly.

Mockin's Catchin': Superstitious warning not to mimic anyone with unfortunate circumstances lest a similar fate may result.

'Mon You: An attempt to attract someone's attention in order to get them to do something or suffer the consequences.

Moocher: Lethargic person; a scrounger; a footballer who does little but scavenge for goals.

Mooter: Large marble.

Morbs: State of depression.

More Coats Than An Onion: Wearing too much clothing.

More Fises Than The Guilthall Clock: Not very trustworthy; sly and deceitful.

Mortified: Totally embarrased or disgraced.

Mouth: Person who is always boasting or bragging.

Mozzy: Large stone, usually for throwing.

Mucka: Thin moustache.

Mucker: Friend or pal.

Murder: Hard to bear; trouble; very difficult.

Murry Dordy: Mary Doherty.

Myin's: Belonging to me.

Nanchin': Chewing noisily.

Natch: Naturally; of course.

Naw: Negative response.

Nearly Tik The Han' A Ye: Accepted quickly and eagerly before opportunity is lost.

33

Niver Nothin': Disagreement with football referee's decision.

Niver Seen Water: Considered to be dirty.

Newins: Out of the ordinary; a new occurrence.

New Light In The Wunda: Something unusual or surprising.

Newrp: Nag or nuisance.

Nickie Cakes: Large plain biscuits; very easy.

Nippin': Very cold.

No Harm Ti' Ye: This will probably upset you (usually precedes an uncomplimentary remark).

No Heat That Day: It's cold today.

Not A Bit Backward About Comin' Forward: Not very shy; outgoing.

Not A Boul In The Dresser: Totally toothless.

Not A Broken Bit: In good condition.

Not Asked If Ye'd A Mouth On Ye: Not offered any food or drink on a visit.

Not A Thing In: No shopping done; nothing to offer a visitor.

Not At Yurself: Unwell; sick.

Not A Wane Washed: Nothing achieved, completed or carried out.

Not Half Wise: Capable of strange behaviour.

Nothin' Strange Or Startlin'? Hello.

Nothin' Wud Do Ye: You had to have it your own way; you deserve it.

Not Interruptin' Your Discourse: Excuse me for butting in.

Not In With: Out of favour with.

Not Worth Tuppence: Taken weak or very nervous; useless.

Och, Dear Aye: I agree totally.

Och, God Wuz Good Ti' 'Im: Usually said of someone who has just died in agony.

Och, You're All Right Sure: No thanks.

Odd: Disinclined to speak; eccentric; moody.

Odd As Two Lefts: Very eccentric.

Odds: Spare change in pocket.

Oney: Only.

Oul Cryba: One who is easily upset or complains for no reason.

Oul Fashioned: Devious; sly; set in one's ways.

Oul Granny Grunt: Reference to a child too advanced for its years.

Oul Lick: Someone who tries to curry favour with another.

Oul Rip: Gossiping woman; trouble maker.

Over The Ways: Vague directional advice.

Oxter: Armpit.

Pallatic: Intoxicated to the point of immobility.

Pantwatchin': Spying on courting couples.

Pass Yurself: Give reasonable account; not disgrace yourself.

Peggin' Breeks: Throwing stones.

Petted Lip: On the verge of tears; huffing.

Pewmoaney: Disease of the lungs.

35

Physic: Laxative.

Piece: Slice of bread; a sandwich.

Piggin': Very dirty (as of house).

Pig Ignernt: Very rude or bad mannered.

Plague: Person intensely disliked.

Plagued: Repeatedly pestered or annoyed.

Pleece: Law officers.

Poke Man: Ice-cream vendor operating from a van.

Poundies: Mixture of mashed potatoes, scallions and butter.

Poyshin: Toxic substance.

Prattie Fadge: Potato bread.

Prodisin: Non-Catholic.

Prog: Steal apples from an orchard.

Puddin': Someone not very good at football; generally useless person.

Puke: Unsavoury character; to throw up.

Put A Bush In Thon Gap: Close the door.

Putrid: Not up to standard; rotten.

Put The Blah On: Curse; bring bad luck upon.

Quare Gunk: Bitter shock or disappointment.

Quare Han' At: Good at the job; dexterous.

Quare 'N' Saft: Not at all queer or soft; not to be believed.

Quare Packin': Good food; filling meal.

Quare Colour: Having a good suntan.

Quet It: Stop now; give it up; desist.

Ragin': Very angry or upset.

Ramscootrify: Completely destroy (usually applied to a person).

Rare Boy/Duck: Eccentric person.

Rare Up On: Take issue with; scold; give off to.

Reach Fur: Physically attack.

Ready Fur The Hills: At wit's end; approaching breaking point.

Redd: Clean up; tidy away.

Red'ner: Blushing; highly embarrassed.

Reel: Idiot; fool.

Rench: Rinse with water.

Ringln': Soaking wet.

Rooked: Left without money; usually as a result of gambling.

Rotton Wi' Dough: Affluent; well-to-do.

Royit: Civil disturbance.

Ructions: Uproar; general melee.

Ruined: Very badly spoiled (as of a child).

Rumberella: Device for deflecting rain.

Saft Ca: Do you really think I believe what you're saying?

Saftee, Wud Ye Eat A Brick?: You're not so stupid.

Saft Mark: Person easily deceived or taken in.

Santy: Father Christmas.

Say Nothin' Ti' Ye See Claude: Refrain from talking until you consult a solicitor; plead innocent.

Scobe: Eat with gusto.

Scobie: Turnip.

Sconcin': Staying away from school without consent.

Scootie Hole: Gap in hedge or fence.

Score: The act of attracting a member of the opposite sex.

Scorrick: Odds and ends in a pocket; the last dregs of a cigarette.

Scotchie: Type of Scout's lift using the hands to help a friend over a wall.

Scrake A Dawn: First light.

Scran: Small amount of money (or possessions) gained by dubious means; the scant remains of anything.

Screenge: Search frantically for money or other essentials.

Scrippin': Scratching sound.

Scrippins: Leftovers; dregs.

Scrunch: Squash; crunch.

'Scuse Me Fur Breathin': Sorry I opened my mouth

Seepin': Very wet.

See Ye After: Cheerio.

Sent Fur (I Thought I Wuz): Dead.

Set: On the road to success.

Shade: Small building in the backyard used for storing materials or working in.

Sheely Wi' The Wee Girls: Boys should be boys.

Shipquay Street's A Slippy Street Ti' Slide Upon: Dangerous Derry tongue twister.

Shoogly Shoo: Type of swing in children's playground.

Shootie In: Football game in which everybody has a free shot at the nets.

Shot Down: A loser in love.

Silly Bugle: Person who does something stupid.

Simmit: A vest.

Sit At Peace: Command to child to desist from annoying activity.

Sittin' In The Middle A Me Dinner: In the process of eating lunch.

Sittin' Wi' A Fis On: Looking bad tempered or depressed.

Siz Who? Inquiry as to where recently communicated information came from.

Skahy: Messy meal of unusual ingredients.

Skelligan/Skellington: The bony framework of the body.

Skelly: Vision slightly askew; cross-eyed.

Skelp/Skite: Sharp slap.

Skunnered: Greatly dispirited.

Slabber: Loudmouth; unlikeable person.

Slabbers: Saliva drooling from mouth.

Slag: To make disparaging comments about someone.

Sleekid: Sly; devious; dishonest.

Slip The Backs: Get away; get off lightly.

Smidgin': A small amount.

Smittle: Contagious.

Smoothe: To iron clothes.

Snotterbox: Nose.

So Am Are: I certainly am.

Sola: A card game for one.

Sore Hand: Large piece of bread with butter and jam.

Sore Head: Type of plain pastry.

Sore On Ye: Sympathetic remark when one is treated badly or unjustly.

Sound: Just fine; perfect; dependable; trustworthy.

Sound Affair: Good idea; expression of agreement.

Speel: To climb up.

Spit Out Or Ye'll Grow Horns: Advice given to children after they've bumped heads.

Spittin': Beginning to rain.

Spla-Futted: Having flat, broad feet positioned at a wide angle to each other.

Split: To open a wound in someone's head.

Spoilt Rotten: Very pampered (of child).

Sprasie: Sixpence in "old" money.

Stacks: Lots of; plenty.

Stand In: Take shelter from the rain.

Standin' Lik A Lilty: Looking very silly and embarrassed.

Standin' Wi' Yur Two Arms The Wan Length: Looking stupid and out of place.

Start (Someone): Provoke a person to fight.

Starvin': Very cold or hungry.

Stews: Food in general - mince, potatoes, onions and carrots in particular.

Stickin' Out: Wonderful; great.

Stocious/Stovin': Highly intoxicated.

Stop It Ah Luv It: Jovial resistance to cuddling.

Stroop: Spout of kettle or teapot.

Stump: Core or remains of half-eaten apple.

Suck The Butts: Person who tries to get as many puffs as possible from a cigarette.

Swappin' Spittles: Kissing.

Sweel: Wind round and round.

Sweem: Propel oneself through water using the arms and legs.

Swiddies: Confectionery of all sorts.

Swipe: Steal.

Swizz: Playfully spinning a child round and round very quickly.

Talent: Available girls sought by eager boys or vice versa.

Tank: Sum total of all money owned (and about to be squandered).

Tant: Tempt or taunt.

Tap: Beg or borrow money.

Tap Up: Ask to leave a girl or boy home.

Tartles: Raggedy clothes; knots in hair.

Tay: An addictive drink made from the dried shredded leaves of an Asian shrub and hot water.

That Crowd: Usually adverse reference to all government bodies.

That'll Fatten Ye: That won't fatten you at all - nor will it benefit you.

That'll Niver Buy The Wane A Coat: That's not much good.

That's A Sin: You shouldn't be doing whatever it is you're doing.

The Balls A Me Legs Are Turned To The Front: My legs are very sore.

The Blether's Niver Far From Yur Eyes: You're always near to tears.

The Bror: My brother.

The Cat Can Luk At The King: Sharp retort to the question "what are you looking at?"

The Cruelty Man: Person responsible for child welfare.

The Gimmeys: Affliction that makes people (especially children) keep asking for things.

The Gravy's Lashin' A Me: I'm very hot; I'm sweating profusely.

The Hen That Laid Them Must've Had Stays On: Those eggs are rather small.

The Holy Man's Name: A religious oath.

The Kinda Me: The type of person I am.

Them Cups Have Beards On Them: That china needs washing.

The Messages: The groceries; shopping.

Themins: Those people.

The Morra: The day after today.

Them There: Those.

The Nash: National assistance - a type of unemployment benefit no longer in use.

There'll Be Two Blue Moons In The Sky An' Wan In The Dungpit: That's unlikely to occur.

There's Me Han' Up Ti' God: I swear it's the truth.

There's More Beef On A Coul Chip: I've seen better built people.

There's Wiser In Lukin' Out: A belief that someone is not in full control of their senses.

The Things Ye See When Ye Haven't A Gun: Jovial insult on a chance meeting with an old friend.

The Two Mahoods: Two friends or associates who are always together.

They'd Tik The Bite Out A Yur Mouth: They're greedy people.

Thick As Poundies: Stupid.

Thon: That thing.

Thonder: Over there.

Thon Wan: That person.

Thran: Obstinate; hard to shift.

Thrapple: Throat or Adam's apple.

Threatenin' Letter: Written notification from the labour exchange (Jobmarket) about a job.

Tick: Credit given in shops etc.

Tie The Boy: Character renowned for his untidy manner of dress.

Tik The Bare Luk Off: Do something to divert attention from; to dress something up a bit.

Tik The Break Off: Create distraction to lessen the embarrassment.

Tik The Heart From Ye: Compliment on noticing an appetising aroma.

Tik The Rough Off: Give a light cleaning; spruce up slightly.

Tik Yur Shade: To pinch the nose and dip the head backwards under the water when swimming. (Said by children.)

Till (The Door): Push the door ajar.

Tilly: Daily Belfast newspaper.

Tip's Yur Keek: Game of street football in which even a slight touch of the ball is considered a kick.

Tortured: Repeatedly irritated by another's behaviour.

Tossie Pit: Group of people gambling by flipping coins in the air.

Trail: Fight; drag along by the hair.

Trimendus: Great; excellent.

Trimmlin': Shaking with fear or cold.

Trumf: Trumps (as in cards).

Tube: Derogatory name for a useless person.

Tube 'N' Cover: Old style soccer ball.

Tuffy: Hard confectionery.

Tuk Bad: Became ill.

Tuk Wake: Felt faint; overcome with sickness or nerves.

Tummle: Topple over.

Turmit: Large root vegetable.

Turn Round: Begin, usually unfavourably.

Two's Up On Ye: Request for smoke of cigarette.

Two Wanses: Two tossed coins landing one heads and the other tails.

41

Up A Tree In Rosemount: Missing but not missed; whereabouts unknown, absence unlamented.

Up Ti' Belfast: Down to Belfast.

Usual Oul Toot: Same old story.

Vepes: V.P. wine.

Vile: Awful.

Wadgin: Big, shapeless piece of something.

Wait An' I'll Dance Ti' Ye: I certainly will not do as you ask.

Walter: Play around in mud or dirt.

Wan: One.

Wanebitter: Person who picks fights with kids.

Wanes: Children.

Wan's Errand: Fruitless message.

Waster: A good-for-nothing individual.

Watch The Grittins: Helpful but teasing advice to thin person.

Watch Ye Don't Heat Yur Water: Sarcastic remark to slowcoach.

Water Biscuits: Cream crackers.

Water Brash: Indigestion; sour acid from stomach.

Wee Buns: Very easy; no problem.

Wee Critter: Expression of sympathy for suffering child or animal.

Wee Dote: Compliment to a cute baby; term of endearment used by a girl about a good-looking boy.

Wee Hard: Small tough person.

Weemin: Adult females.

Wee Minute: Short period of time; normally longer than a minute.

Ween: A small number; a few.

Wee Nadger: Youngest or smallest child.

Wee Nuns: Primary school in the vicinity of the Long Tower Church, Derry.

Wee Sope/Drop In Yur Han': Quick drink of tea offered to a visitor, not in the hand but in a cup.

Wee Tist: A little of anything.

Wee Want: Something missing mentally in a person.

Wee Way A Workin': Routine peculiar to each individual.

We Know Ye: Smug remark made when someone's darkest secret is discovered.

We Know Ye Are: You are not.

Well At: Wealthy.

Well Away: Going great; doing very well.

Well Mended: Having put on weight; physically improved.

Were Ye Born In A Field? Close the door.

Whaddy Ye Think It Is – Christmas? No, you can't have it.

What About Ye, Kid? Warm greeting to a good friend.

What Did Yur Last Skivvy Die Of? Do it yourself.

What Iver Ye Say, Say Nothin': Warning to be cautious in conversation lest confidential information should escape.

What's The Crack? Any news? What's happening?

When Yur Han's In: Now that you've got the hang of it.

Where's Yur Office? Mind your own business; don't try to boss me about.

Whisperin' Man: Mysterious character, infamous for knocking at (or peeping in) people's windows.

Wile: Very; terrible.

Wine Victim: Sad name for a person who's too fond of cheap alcohol.

Wing: One penny in "old" money.

Wi'out A Dollion: Completely naked.

Wiped: Having dole money stopped in contentious circumstances.

Wired Up Ti' The Moon: Psychologically disturbed.

Wile Big Eyed: Greedy.

Wile Blowey: Windy; blowing a gale.

Wile Civil: Good-mannered; decent type.

Wile Colour: Sick-looking; having a pale complexion.

Wile Dose: A cold or flu.

Wile Good Livin': Leading a pious life.

Wile Lukin': Ugly.

Wile Man: Mischievous, unpredictable, devil-may-care person.

Wile Strange: Child who doesn't take to strangers.

Wile Tik A Han': Person who plays tricks on, or makes fun of, others.

Wise Up, Wull Ye? Have some sense.

Wo, Beek: Command for horse to stop.

Won't Try A Leg: Makes no attempt at all; lazy.

Wooden Overcoat: Coffin.

Worked Wi': Brought round; helped to recover after a shock or accident.

Work In: Get some overtime on the job.

Worser: Worse again.

Wrecked: Extremely embarrassed.

Wreck The House: Name for clumsy person; cheap wine.

Wudda Woman: Widow.

Wudn't Give Ye The Itch: Very stingy.

Wudn't Turn The Word In Yur Mouth: Very docile; wouldn't argue back.

Wud Ye Be Guilty? You wouldn't catch me doing that.

Wud Ye Tik Me Grave As Quick? Question asked when someone "steals" another's seat.

Wulla? Will I?

Wulwurs: Large department store in central Derry.

Ye Could Grow Spuds In Yur Ears: Why don't you wash yourself more often?

Wunda: Window.

Wunst: One time.

Wur: Our.

Wurl: Wheel along; spinning wildly.

Ye Couldn't Break Ye Wi' A Sledgehammer: You're not easily embarrassed.

Ye Couldn't Draw The Bru: You're not a very good artist.

Ye Couldn't Hear Yur Ears: It was too noisy.

Ye Couldn't Lik 'Im If He Wuz Made A Chocolate: He's hateful.

45

Ye Couldn't See Green Cheese But Yur Mouth Waters: You're a very greedy person.

Ye'd Get Redd A Yur Smell That Day: It's very windy outside today.

Ye'd Luk Well: You'd look very foolish.

Ye'd Need A Pixie On Ye That Weather: It's a very cold day.

Ye Have Two Chances: You've no chances at all.

Ye Know: You don't know – that's why I'm telling you.

Ye Know What I Mean, Lik? Do you get the message?

Ye'll Hit Whose Granny Wi' A Wine Bottle? Jocular remark to mock threat against one's female ancestor.

Ye Missed It: You should have been there for the merriment and other wonderful goings-on.

Ye Niver Know You're Livin' Ti' Ye Luk At Yur Shirt: You learn something new every day.

Ye Remember Yur Granny Well: You've got a good memory.

Yer Man: Him.

Yes: Puzzling answer to unasked question, used as a greeting when one Derry person meets another.

Ye Say More Than Yur Prayers: You're nothing but a bluffer.

Yes, Boss: Greeting to someone who's not your employer.

Ye Tell Me That, Aye? I'm not sure if I believe you.

Ye've Got Yur Gittins: You've had enough; you're getting no more.

You'd Kill Dead Things: You're all talk and no action.

You'd Lik Ti' Know: I'm not telling you.

You'll Dear Buy It: You're in for it; there's trouble brewing.

You're A Good Turn: What do you take me for? Do you expect me to believe you?

You're A Liar: You don't say - tell me some more.

You're As Lazy As Sin: Said to someone who's adverse to work.

You're A Teller: I know you don't really work in a bank, but is what you've just said true?

You're Away Wi' The Fairies: Out of touch with reality.

You're Better Ravin' There Than In Yur Bed: You're talking nonsense.

You're Excused But You're Dammed Ignernt: Expression of mocking forgiveness.

You're Funny But Yur Fis Beats Ye: That's not a bit funny.

You're Laughin': You're home and dry; success is imminent.

You're Lukin' Well, Were Ye Lyin'? You look terrible, what happened to you?

You're No Dozer: It would be difficult to fool you.

You're Not On: Nothing doing; no way!

You're Standin' In Me Light: Stop blocking my view.

Youse/Yousins: You people.

You Sicken' My Happiness: I find you very annoying.

You've A Neck On Ye: You've got quite a nerve; you're very cheeky.

You Wud Know: You would not know.

Yur Eye's Out: You've no chance; someone else will beat you to it.

Yur Granny Wuz Doherty (An' She Wuz The Blood): Regardless of who your granny was, you're wrong.

Yur Head's A Marley: I think you've reached an incorrect conclusion; you're talking rubbish.

Yur Head's Cut: I disagree with you.

Yur Wants Wud Make A Poor Man Rich: There's no pleasing you.

Spisser

THE wile BIG DERRY PHRASEBOOK

THE FOLLY UP

DERRY CHARACTERS

Chalk 'N' Water: Allegedly sold water and chalk as milk from a cart.

Danny McDaid: Fanatical Derry City supporter who used to turn his back and shuffle his feet when Derry were under pressure.

Danny Wan Eye And Rosie: Could be seen any Saturday night fighting the bit out and lived in old Springtown Camp.

Gacka Wacka: Victim of over-fondness for alcohol.

Gleek At The Moon: Had some neck ailment, so appeared to be permanently looking at the sky.

Hawker Lynch: Edward J. Lynch was a familiar sight on the streets of the city with his sandwich board covered in advertisements, and at soccer matches, where he sold raffle tickets.

Johnny Cutthims: Drooled a little and sold the Evening Press.

Johnny The German: Former resident of the Wells area, origin of name uncertain.

Maggie McCay: Always dressed in black shawl and dark clothes; reputedly (but doubtfully) a witch.

Micky Hallstand: Came from the Lone Moor Road area. Got his name because his coat always appeared to be half hanging off him.

Slabbery Mickey: Little man who gathered rags and jampots. Drooled somewhat, hence the name.

Smokey Rogers: Came from Ferguson's Lane and had a voice like a foghorn, though most of what he said was difficult to comprehend.

Stephen: Eccentric character known to do odd things e.g. carry a lorry chassis on his old bike.

Tipperary: A great street entertainer who unfortunately fell victim to drink and died relatively young.

Wabbits: Character who hung around the quay, pushing a bike laden down with scrap and bits and pieces.

Walk-A-Bike: Charles George O'Brien, an eccentric solicitor who never went anywhere without a bicycle but never actually rode on it.

DIFFERENCES OF OPINION

A Bunch A Fives: A fistful of knuckles, usually administered forcefully.

Al Bust Yur Head: Threat of impending violence.

Al Dance On Ye: You're asking for trouble.

Al Do Ye: Take yourself off before I beat you up.

Al Go Thru Ye Lik A Dose A Salts: I'd advise you to leave immediately.

Al Hiv Ye, Mucker: Swords or pistols?

Al Pan Ye: I'll thump your head.

Al Spit In Yur Eye: I detest you.

Al Swing On Ye: Threat of violence from female to male.

Aye, You An Whose Army? Derisive response to threat of attack.

Bitt The Linin Outta: Give a severe beating to.

Bleenge: Massive swinging blow.

Bline Swipe: Wild swing with fist at some part of another's anatomy.

Brain: Inflict serious injury on someone's head with a heavy implement.

Cuttin Up Rough: Just about to be violent.

De Ye Want Yur Head In Yur Hands? Direct challenge to opponent.

Eat: Violently take issue with.

Git Scripped: Go away; you're not on.

Go An Tik A Runnin Jump: Uncompromising term of refusal.

Quare Dig: Painful body blow.

Stikkit: Instant comment on being refused share of something.

The Laugh'll Bay On The Oller Side Ay Yur Fis: I would advise you to stop smirking.

Wile Keekin: A serious beating.

Ye Cudn't Bitt Yur Way Out Ay A Pipper Bag: You're not exactly the world's greatest fighter.

Yure Fur Nawhin: You're completely useless – a waster.

BARS AND BOOZE

A Munk Bay The Neck: A bottle of beer.

Are Ye Stanin? Broad hint to another to buy a drink.

Blarge: Large amount of drink.

Blootered: Very intoxicated.

Christian Bror: A bottle of Guinness.

Futliss: Walking erratically due to excess alcohol.

Half Cut/Tubed: On the way to drunken bliss.

Half 'N' A Bottle: Standard Derry order in a pub.

On The Tear/Rip: An extended drinking session.

Outta Yur Mind: In an alcohol-induced world of one's own.

Palatic: In a different universe.

Porter-Belly: Overweight through consuming too much black beer.

Scootered: The alcoholic level below 'blootered'.

Stovin: Pretty drunk.

Wee Hot Half: A measure of whiskey and hot water.

Wee Tritt: A little drink on a special occasion.

Well-On: Three-quarters-way drunk.

CHILDHOOD DELICACIES

In the heady days before frenetic mutant sea creatures and pizzas inhabited the world, children of all ages took their few old pence pocket money to the corner shop to treat themselves. Available there was a small but exciting selection of down-to-earth 'sweeties' which always tasted great and seemed to last all day. Such were the days of innocence and simplicity, expectation and hope, and childhood delicacies. How many can you remember?

Aniseed Balls
Banana Splits
Bazookas
Blackjacks
Brandy Balls
Broken Biscuits
Bubbley Gum
Carmels
Chewing Gum Balls
Danny Boys
Everlasting Strip
Fizz
Flying Saucers
Gobstoppers
Goldmines
Ha'penny Chix

Jube Jubes
Liquorice Pipes
Liquorice Sticks
Love Hearts
Lucky Bags
Lucky Dips
Peggy's Leg
Penny Dainties
Pineapple Chunks
Puff Candy
Spangles
Sweetie Fags
Sweetie Tobacco
Toffee Apples
Whoppers

MARLEY RULES

Bendy Knocks: I can hit opponent's marble to restart game if third person has gained an advantage.

Drops: You have to drop your marble on mine from shoulder height with your eyes closed.

Everyhing And Nawhin: I can do what I like, but you have to wait a turn.

High Drops/Heights: You must drop your marble on mine from as high a position as possible.

High Scoots: You have to scoot your marble down on mine from a great height.

Layin: I don't have to throw my marble up to the mug (hole) if I don't want to.

Long Scoots: You have to scoot your marble at mine from a great distance off.

Mug: Hole into which marble is directed.

Mugs: I can throw my marble into the hole.

No Dibs: You're not allowed to hit my marble.

No Reddins: I can put whatever I like in front of my marble so you can't hit it.

Reddins: I'm allowed to clear away all obstacles in order to get a better shot at your marble.

Scoots: You have to propel your marble rapidly with your thumb against your finger.

Skees On: I'm allowed to strike an opponent's marble and use it to hit another person's marble.

Squarins: I can move around in a circular motion to get a better shot at your marble.

FOOTBALL FLAK

Av A Wane In The House Who Cud Keek A Ball Harder: Comment on half-hearted play.

Ay Cudn't Save Ciggies: Gordon Banks he's not.

Big Git: Large attendance at a match.

C'mon Badgerovitch: Overheard at Derry City v Red Star Belgrade game.

C'mon Derry, Skin Em: Supporters' rallying call.

Dig A Hole: Unsympathetic remark shouted when member of opposing team is injured.

Don't Send Im Aff, Ref, He's The Best Man We've Got: Subtle criticism of whole team effort.

Give That Ref A Blue/Green/Red Etc Jersey: Accusation of bias against match official.

Hi, Hiv Ye A Hole In Yur Fut Ur What? That wasn't a very accurate pass.

Hi, Ref, De Ye Wan A Lenna May Glasses? That was definitely a misjudgement.

Hi, Ref, Did Ye Swally Yur Wussle Ur What? Why didn't you detect that foul play?

His Laces Must Be Tied Tigether Or Sumfin: Said about uncoordinated player.

Houl On Ti It, It'll Be A Better Match Wi'out It: Remark passed when ball is kicked into the crowd.

May Granny Cuda Saved That Wan And She's Oney Got Wan Arm: Somewhat unkind comment made about incompetent goalie.

Movin Stychays: Sarcastic reference to inactive Derry City players.

No Wonder Ye Spend Most Of Yur Time On The Bench: You're little asset to the team.

Shower A Slabbers: Unfortunate Derry opposition.

Wipe-O: Encouragement from fans to player to adopt unsavoury tactics.

Ye Cudn't Catch A Coul: Why do you keep dropping the ball?

Ye Cudn't Cross Yur Legs: Judgement made on poor passer.

Ye Cudn't Pick Yur Nose: I disagree with your (the manager's) choice of players.

Ye Cudn't Run A Message: Incisive judgement made on slow player.

FOOD AND DRINK

A Drop A Tay: Light hot refreshment.

Baps: Tasty round buns, nice with butter.

Brackfist: First meal in the morning.

Brocken: Porridge oats.

Chesterbred: Thick square bun made from dubious ingredients (also known as a sinker).

Chookie: Chicken.

Crips: Multi-flavoured fried potato slices.

Cuttin Loaf: Yesterday's bread, bought when times were hard.

Ditts: Exotic fruit from the East.

Hern: Salty fish containing thousands of bones.

Injin Mail: Type of reddish-coloured porridge oats.

Lemmanade: Mixture of water, sugar and gas with a variety of flavours.

Lofa Brown: One unit of wheaten bread.

Swuss Roll: Rolled-up spongy pastry filled with jam.

Tamada: Red seedy fruit used in salads and sandwiches.

Turnover: Diamond-shaped bun with blob of jam in the middle.

Wiffer: Two thin rectangular biscuits with ice-cream in between them.

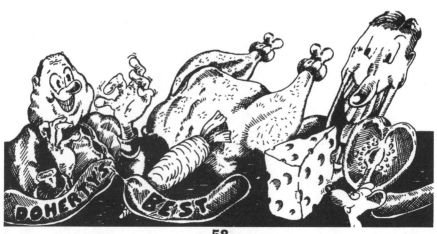

FAMOUS DERRY PLACES (PAST AND PRESENT)

Altygalvin: Derry's main hospital.

Back Of The Wall: Nailor's Row/ Walker's Square area, now demolished.

The Back Stores: Alleyway that once went from Little James Street to William Street.

Bap's: Battisti's Cafe, once situated in Ferryquay Street.

The Basin: Creggan Reservoir.

The Big House: The old asylum on the Strand Road.

The Bloods: Old dancehall in the Bogside.

Breeze Lane: Road between Lone Moor Road and Creggan.

Bridge Street University: Little school in Bridge Street, now closed.

Bucket Of Blood: Public house infamous for brawls, once situated at Bishop's Gate.

The Bug Ranch: Old City Cinema once in William Street.

The Bull: Area on the Lone Moor Road.

The Byewash: Little waterfall between Rosemount and Glenowen.

Cannibal Island: Rinmore Drive in Creggan.

The Close: Small street once situated in the Rossville Street area.

The Corbie: Roundabout at junction of Central Drive and Westway.

The Dark Lane: Small street once in the Long Tower area, now demolished.

The Donkey/Daisy Fields: Grassy areas in the Brandywell area.

The Dump: Football pitch in the Brandywell area.

Egglington: Picturesque village not far from Derry.

The Five Lamps: Toilets once in Waterloo Place, now demolished.

The Fryin Pan: Small pub once situated on the Lone Moor Road.

Futta Stanley's: At the bottom of Stanley's Walk, a street in the Bogside.

The Gashyard: The former gasworks over the Lecky Road.

The Gorbals: The Waterside.

Grazy Barney's: Little fish and chip shop once situated in William Street.

Greenhell: Springtown Camp which is no longer in existence.

The Heights: The top end of the Creggan Estate.

Hogg's Folly: Steep winding street in the Long Tower area.

Holy Rosemount: Area situated near Creggan Estate.

Ivy House: The tall leaning red-bricked building beside the Strand Cinema.

Jerusalem: Meenan Park.

Molly On The Moor: Second-hand shop that used to be on the Lone Moor Road.

The Threepenny Bits: Stone fixtures that used to be in front of the Rossville Street flats.

Thran John's: Public house in Shantallow.

Thunderin Down: Narrow lane off Lone Moor Road, now demolished.

Top Of The Hill: Gobnascale.

Treacle Hole's: Shop in Central Drive.

Up The Bankin: Grassy slope between the Bogside and Derry's Walls.

Up The Bog: Somewhere in the Bogside.

Up The Boleyays: Area in Waterside associated with romantic assignations.

Wee Johnny's: Old-fashioned 'sweetie shop' that used to be in Bishop Street.

The Workhouse: Grim building which is now the old Waterside hospital.

Above All Days: Why did it have to happen today?

Actin The Maggot/Wack: Behaving in an annoying manner.

Actin Up: Not playing the game; misbehaving; machinery malfunctioning.

Ageein: Once more.

Ageenst: Strongly opposed to.

Aggervittin: Causing severe annoyance and frustration.

Ah Canny Bay Footered: I can't be bothered; it's too much trouble.

Ah Canny Git Lukin Outta May Eyes: Gasp of despair by harrassed parent.

Ah Haddy: I felt compelled to; I had to.

Ah Hadn't An Eye In May Head: Condition brought about by too much looking, reading, or too little sleep.

Ah Hivn't A Han On May: Condition caused by person overworking.

Ah Hivn't A Sausage/Tosser: I'm financially embarrassed; completely penniless.

Ah Need Thing: I'm running short.

Ah Niver Laughed So Many Since Ah Wuz A Wee Children In A Cot: I was falling about in stitches.

Ah Went Up The Stairs An Threw Maysel Down: I felt rather tired, so I went to bed for a while.

Ah Wudn't Put It Past Ye: I don't trust you; you're capable of doing something devious or underhand.

Alameenyum: Silvery coloured metal used for making teapots etc.

Al Bibbildy Gore: I'm free to visit you later.

Al Draw The Back A May Han Across Yur Ja'bone: Dire threat by parent against child that chastisement is imminent.

Al Give Ye Sumfin Ti Cry About: Threat of further punishment if child doesn't desist from crying.

Al Gup An Throw On May: I'll go upstairs and get dressed.

All Ears: Listening intently; eavesdropping.

All Pitcher An No Soun: Frosty atmosphere prevailing when wife/girlfriend isn't speaking to husband/boyfriend(or vice versa).

Al Warm Yur Ear: Warning from parent to offspring to behave or else.

Am Bitt: I'm defeated; I give up; I'm totally exhausted.

Am G'inout: Cheerio, I've decided to go somewhere else.

Am Niver Goney: Cry of desperation when failure looms.

Am Not Goney Eat It On Ye: Angry retort when someone is refused permission to look at something belonging to another.

Am Not Goney Run Outta The Town Wi It, Ye Know: Indignant retort when someone is reminded that they've got a minor outstanding debt.

Am Not Yur Skivvy: Do it yourself.

Am Ready Fur The Big House: I think I'm going mad.

Am Rotton So Am Are: I've definitely got a very bad dose of the cold.

Am Survivin: It's a struggle, but I'll manage.

Amup: I've arisen out of my bed.

Am Wile Sarry: Please forgive me, I apologise.

Anacordjin: Musical instrument with piano keyboard and bellows.

A Nearly Tuk Duck Disease: I almost went into a state of shock.

Any Wan Not Wearin A Coat That Day Hasn't Got Wan: It's extremely cold today.

Ar: Livid mark left after wound has healed.

Arthuritus: Disease that causes pain and inflammation in the joints.

Artickilated Larry: Heavy goods vehicle.

As God Is May Judge: I wouldn't lie to you (even though I am).

As Good: Very kind; generous.

Ask May Bror Am I A Liar: Seeking questionable confirmation of one's honesty.

As Oul As Tay: Advanced in years; aged.

Aw Dear O: Sign of exasperation.

Aw, God Luv Thim: Expression of sympathy for innocent children.

Aw, Wudn't Ye Know? Smug remark when informed of another's misdeed.

Ay Cudn't Cure Bacon: My doctor is a bit of a quack.

Aye, Right Anuff: Get lost, do you think I'm an idiot?

Back Return: Extension to rear of house.

Baddin: Person inclined to bouts of anti-social behaviour; mischievous child.

Bad Scran/Cess Ti Ye: I wish you all the worst.

Bags: Garments covering the lower half of a man.

Ball A Lard: Most unkind remark about obese person.

Banana Slide: Item of recreation in children's playground.

Bankin: Steep grassy incline.

Barred: Prohibited from entering place of entertainment because of past (mis)behaviour.

Batterin Match: Over-enthusiastic knocking at door.

Beetle: Wooden, club-shaped implement for mashing potatoes.

Big Fis: Insult of medium seriousness; facial expression denoting huffing.

Big Long Drink A Watter/String A Misery: Tall gangly useless person.

Big People: Adults; grown-ups.

Bissin: Metal or plastic container for washing dishes in.

Bit Ay A Boy: Not averse to chasing the ladies; a man about town.

Bitta Stuff: Dubious male comment about an attractive female.

Bitter: Very cold.

Bitt Ti The Ropes: Completely overwhelmed; last chance gone; penniless.

Black: Chock-a-block with people.

Black Bibbies: Unfortunate children of the Third World for whom collections are taken up in schools.

Black Stranger: A totally unknown person.

Blellerin: Talking loudly in a moaning or complaining manner.

Bline: Unable to see.

Blissin: Benevolent bestowing of good fortune by the Almighty.

Bokeyman: Nebulous scary character from children's nightmares usually conjured up by parents to enforce discipline.

Bollerayshun: Tedious task; too much like work.

Boul Cut: Child's hairstyle achieved by expert use of a soup bowl and scissors (usually in hard times).

Boulster: Large elongated pillow.

Boult: Type of sliding lock for door.

Bounchin: Rebounding continuously off the ground or wall.

Brack In Ti: Enter illegally.

Brattle: Loud peal of thunder.

Brock: Leftover household food once collected in carts and used to feed pigs.

Brockman: Man with horse and cart who collected brock.

Bunnle: Bunch of material tied with string (e.g. bunnle a sticks).

Burnt Offerin: Overcooked food presented as meal.

Burry: Inter; stow away in the ground.

Burton's Dummy: Person who doesn't over-exert himself; overdressed and awkward.

Bust Out: Be overcome by a paroxysm of laughing or crying.

Butter Wudn't Melt In Er Mouth An A Poun Wudn't Choke Er: She's not as innocent as she would have you believe.

Calendar: Container full of holes for straining food.

Catch: Not as good as it's made out to be; a con trick.

Change Yursel: Put on a new set of clothes.

Chawin: Eating noisily.

Chessy: Fruit of the chestnut tree used for playing conkers.

Chest Lik A Fourpenny Rabbit: A bit on the thin side.

Chiss: Pursue; run after; see off pronto.

Choon Gum: Obnoxious sticky stuff chewed by people of a nervous disposition.

Chronic: Terrible; awful.

Chuck It Out: Desist immediately, you're annoying me.

Civil Bein: Well-mannered agreeable sort of person.

Clean Mit Niver Fattened A Pig: Admonishment to person who's over-particular about food hygiene.

Comin Back Ti Yursel: Looking better; more like your old self.

Conscrew: Apply a meaning to someone's words at variance with what was intended.

Coo-Coo: Hello, here I am (usually addressed to child).

Corinthian Crawl: Type of shuffling dance supposed to have originated in the old Corinthian ballroom.

Corner Boy: Layabout; one who loiters around the streets all day.

Coul: Not warm.

Coul Showlder: What you get when you're completely ignored; a brushoff.

Cozzie: Half a brick or large stone.

Crab: Argument provoker; disgruntled type.

Crack's Ninety: We're having a jolly good time.

Cribbin: Moaning or complaining.

Crissanin: Church service where baby is given its name by having water poured on its head.

Cruel: Very bad; hard to take (as of performer).

Cryin Jas: Complaining type; weepy child.

Curly: Type of vegetable.

Dancin: Hopping mad with rage.

Daygeller: All at the same time; in a group.

Deep: Mysterious; descriptive of someone who thinks a lot.

De Ye Know Yure Livin? For God's sake, shake yourself.

De Ye Want Jam On It? There's no satisfying you.

Die Wi Yur Leg Up: Go down fighting.

Diktittin: Laying down the law in no uncertain manner.

Disabejince: Child's unwillingness to do as instructed.

Discombooberate: Destroy; dismantle; completely annihilate.

Disgriss: Utter shame.

Dissint Oul Spud: Kind, generous person (not necessarily old).

Ditt: Romantic rendezvous with member of the opposite sex.

Divilmint: Petty mischief; tomfoolery.

Divour: Violently take to task; severely reprimand.

Diz It Annoy Ye? Why don't you mind your own business.

Do A Bunk: Disappear suddenly without prior notice, abandoning responsibilities or with ill-gotten gains.

Dogged: Mean; nasty; unnecessary act.

Doings: Catch-all word for any forgotten item.

Done Ti The Two Eyeballs: Grossly overcharged; swindled.

Don't Darken The Durr: Never go there again; stay well away.

Don't Spen It All In The Wan Shop: Facetious advice given to recipient of paltry sum of money.

Dotter: Female offspring.

Double Week: Fortnight's dole money, family allowance or wages, depending on circumstances.

Do What The Bees Does - Buzz: Command to go away.

Dragon: Not exactly the most attractive person in the world.

Dressed Up Ti The Nines: Stepping out in style; elegantly attired.

Drooth: Acute, almost unquenchable thirst.

Dry Up An Blow Away: I can't stand you so shut up and leave me alone.

Dunkey: Unkindly reference to message boy in the days of message bikes.

Durrhannle: Metal or wooden appendage on door to assist opening and closing.

Eye Ye Outta Yur Scon Ur Wat? Have you taken leave of your senses? That's a very inadvisable course of action.

Extree Mungshun: Anointment of a person on their death bed by a priest with holy oils.

Edyemicated: Well versed in matters academic; very smart.

Even The Dogs In The Street Know: It's common knowledge.

Eyes 'N' Ears: Someone (especially a child) who hears things they're not supposed to, and isn't likely to keep it to themselves.

Eye Ye Gan Out? Invitation to girl to dance by hopeful suitor.

Fair Lukin Half: Very good-looking woman.

Fair Play Ti Ye: Didn't you do well? Congratulations.

Fall Out Wi: Cease to be on talking terms with a friend.

Famous Fur: Infamous for; having a bad reputation.

Fancy Yursel: Imagining (wrongly) you're a big hit with the opposite sex.

Far Thru: Confused; in a muddle.

Feared: Afraid; scared.

Fihnt: Pass out; lost consciousness.

Fissin: Positioned opposite; face to face.

Floot Me: Oath used by the meek.

Flyer/Flyin Machine: A person (or thing) that moves at great speed (but not a plane).

Folly Up: Pursue to conclusion; a sequel.

For'ner: Person from another country; alien.

Forrid: Part of head just above the eyebrows.

From Flagfall: From the very start.

Full Ay Imself: Preoccupied with his own self-importance.

Galler: Collect together (e.g. galler flowers).

Galler Up: Term for band or football team just thrown together in a hurry, usually for one performance only.

Gammy (Leg): Lame or limping.

Gayvel: End-wall of house.

Geek: Lacking in looks and personality; dullard.

Get: Derogatory name for someone.

Gimme Yur Dandie: Request from mother to child to take her hand.

Git Aff An Push It: Jibe directed at cyclist, especially if bicycle is old.

Git A Grip: Please bring yourself under control.

Git A Wee Run Roun: Pay a quick visit.

Git Fixed Up Wi: Establish a romantic link with.

Git Out The Good Cups: The priest's coming to visit.

Gitta Houlta: To find eventually after a long search.

Git That Durr: Please answer the door.

Git The Haff: Have an unexpected afternoon off school.

Git The Worst Word In Thur Mouth: Be subjected to intense verbal abuse.

Gittin At: Directing one's remarks at somebody while indirectly criticising another.

Gittin Wile Oul: Approaching the latter stages in life.

Gittin Wile Stout: Putting on weight (usually as a result of being pregnant).

Git Yur Feet Under The Tibble: Be invited round to girlfriend's house (regarded cynically as the first step towards marriage).

Git Yur Length: Eventually get around to visiting someone.

Give That Fluer A Lick: The floor needs washing.

Giv'Im A Bib: Isn't he a sloppy eater?

Giv'Is A Bitta That Heat: May I have a seat at the fire please?

Glassy Pipper: Material that Lucozade bottles used to be wrapped in; cellophane.

Go Ahead, Bak Away: Somewhat confusing instruction to vehicle driver to commence reversing.

Go An Tik A Runnin Jump Ti Yursel: Uncompromising term of refusal.

Go A Wee Run: Set off on a short spin in a car.

God Furgimmey This Day: Asking the Lord for absolution for speaking ill of someone (usually in no uncertain terms).

God Luk Ti Ye, Thur's Not A Pik On Ye: Wry comment passed when grossly overweight person complains about the necessity to eat.

God, Yese Are Good Ti Yursels: Criticism of over-indulgent individuals.

G'On Lik: Act in a similar manner; emulate.

Go Haffers: Share equally among two friends (usually when finances are low).

Gone On: Request to proceed.

Good Tist: A fair amount, exact quantity unknown.

Good Thing: Horse or greyhound most likely to come in first.

Gorbal: Person from the Waterside district of Derry.

Gout: To exit the premises.

Gover: Go over.

Govvermint: Group of people who (supposedly) run the country.

Govvermint Artist: One who claims unemployment benefit.

Greatest Thing Since Flemin's Baps/Dordy's Mince: Best invention ever.

Gulf: Refined game played with clubs, balls, tees and holes.

Gulpin: Ill-mannered person; one devoid of breeding.

Gummy: Unkind remark about person short on teeth.

Gumbile: Painful inflamed swelling in mouth.

Gunder: Go below.

Gup: Ascend (e.g. gup the stairs)

Haff Ra: Not very well cooked.

Hairy Wane: Person older than they appear.

Hanks: Thank you; much obliged.

Han Lik A Fut: Oversized appendage; a bad hand at cards.

Hard Ti Whack: Just great; unbeatable.

Harmlis Critter: One who wouldn't hurt a fly; innocuous individual.

Havn't Got Thur Sarras Ti Seek: Having their fair share of trouble.

Hawspittle: Refuge for the sick and injured.

Headbin/Headkis: Person of unpredictable disposition.

Head The Ball: Affectionate title for friend prone to puzzling behaviour.

Heavy Fut: Sound of a big man walking.

Heinz: Mongrel dog.

Heller Kissy: Heather Casey.

Here's Me An Who's Lik May? Sarcasm directed towards person full of self-importance.

He/She Didn't Git That Behine A Stone: Sneering comment that child has inherited adverse traits of one of its parents.

He Wudn't Spend Xmas: He isn't exactly over-extravagant with his money.

Hi Good Lookin - Not You, Hatchet Fiss: Compliment and insult combined (usually a joke).

Hingin: Suspended above the ground.

Hink: Peruse mentally.

Hippiny: Halfpenny in old money.

Hisn't A Baldy: Clueless as to what's happening; stupid.

Hiv A Done Anyhing On Ye? Why do you dislike me so much?

Hiv Up: Legally bring to court over personal slander or other misdeed.

Hiv Ye No Gumshun? You're stupid.

Hiv Yur Eye Wiped: Have the object of your affections stolen from under your nose.

Hope It Chokes Ye: Exclamation of resentment at not being offered share of goodies.

Houl: Hold on to.

Houl Out On: Withhold something from friends that they consider should be evenly shared.

How's The Form, Kid? How are you today?

69

I Ee Yup? Have you risen out of bed yet?

If Ye'd Anyhing In Ye: Remark questioning another's integrity or courage.

Impurvisin: Using unorthodox methods; making the best of what you've got.

In Debt An Danger: In the middle of a financial crisis.

Inglin: Large country across the Irish Sea.

Injin: Front part of train; main component of car.

Istitt: Large area of council houses (e.g. Creggan Istitt).

It's Early In The Day Yit: It's too soon to come to any conclusion and besides, I haven't a clue.

It Jist Shows Ye: You see, you can never be too sure.

It'll Do Ye Rightly: It doesn't matter that you don't want it, you're getting it anyway.

It Tik's Wan Ti Know Wan: Your reputation is suspect as well.

It Won't Bay Long Ti The Mornin, Sure: Don't worry, everything will be all right.

I've A Hannle On May Jug: I've got a Christian name you know.

Iz My Fis Red? Sarcastic answer when someone enquires as to the whereabouts of somebody or something.

Iz That A Threat Ur A Promise? Teasing banter between sexes with suggestive undertones.

Iz That The Nixt Ay It? I can't take any more of this, it's just one thing after another.

Iz Yur Leg Broke Ur Wat? Do it yourself.

Jaggy: Having rough pointed edges.

Jammy: Lucky.

John Shumes: Prominent Derry SDLP politician and MEP.

Joke Wi A Jag In It: Getting a personal rebuke across by dressing it up as comedy.

Juke Down: Protect oneself from danger by dropping to one's knees.

Keep A Wee Eye On/Out: Look after; watch out for.

Keep Goin Ti The Meetins/Tikin The Tablets: You're talking rubbish; frustration is setting in.

Kepp: Retained possession of; continued doing.

Kisser: Mouth or face.

Kiss It Up Ti God: Advice given by one child to another before eating a sweet they've just scraped off the ground.

Knock Yur Pan Out: Toil long and hard for little or no reward.

Kuge: Extremely large; of massive proportions.

Kugo (or Shugo) Kwun: Hugo Quinn.

Kwuns: Five children born of the same mother at the same time.

Lantrin: Portable means of illumination; small lamp.

Latch On Ti: Form unwelcome alliance with.

Laughin An Keh-heyin: Sniggering and muttering in a very annoying manner.

Layin Wide Ti The World: Door left open and unattended.

Lepercorn: Mythical Irish dwarf dressed in colourful clothes.

Less A That An More A The Oller: Jovial resistance to cuddle by member of the opposite sex.

Libberer: Person who toils on building site or does other manual work.

Lidder On: After a while; sometime in the near future.

Lie Down An Die Right: I couldn't care less if you're sick.

Lifted: Arrested, usually in the middle of the night.

71

Lift Yur Han Ti: Make threatening gesture towards, or actually strike, someone.

Lik A Feller: Extremely light; weighing hardly anything.

Lik A Hen Lukin Ore A White-washed Wall: Description of someone (usually wearing glasses) peering from behind something.

Lik An A Promise: A very superficial cleaning.

Lik A Wet Dishcloth: Looking tired and jaded.

Lik Death Warmed Up: A terrible sight altogether.

Lik Nellie Sidebottom: Grossly overweight.

Lik Our Hanna: Unkempt and dirty.

Lik The Scotch Boat: Sound of someone snoring or blowing their nose loudly.

Lissinin: Taking note of what's being said; paying attention.

Liver Lips: Insensitive remark made about someone with an oversized mouth.

Livin Ore The Brush: Cohabiting.

Lizzie Drippin: Affectionate nickname for small child.

Long Chinny: American horror movie actor of yesteryear.

Long Yarn: An awful bore.

Lorn An Harly: Classic American comedy duo.

Low: Mean; underhand.

Lukalik: A person who strongly resembles another.

Lukin Far In Front A Ye: Being too optimistic about the future.

Lukkit The Ship A Ye: Please tidy yourself up.

Luk Over Yur Rentbook, Yure Four Weeks Behind: Derry version of a line from the Eddie Fisher song 'I'm Walking Behind You'.

Luks Lik He Lost A Bob And Found A Tanner: A pessimistic approach to life.

Luk That Wudda Cut Coul Steel: Ominous, threatening stare.

Luk What The Wun Blew In: Friendly greeting to someone not seen for a long time.

Luk What Ye Made May Do Now: I know it's my fault but I have to blame someone else.

Luvly Head A Skin: Light-hearted reference to bald-headed man.

GLEAM

Ma, He's Pullin The Arms Outta The Blankets: Standard Derry joke said to have originated in Springtown Camp where poor people had to use old coats as blankets.

Manky: Of inferior quality; second rate.

Martyr: Long-suffering individual who never receives much sympathy.

Massacray: Slaughter; complete rout.

May Gut's Hingin Outta May: I could be doing with a fish supper.

May Moller: My father's wife.

May The National Assistance Remain Always With Us: Derry 'prayer' playfully praising the virtues of government benefits.

Meejim: Not extreme on one side or another (e.g. meejim rare).

Melder: Terrible mess; loud chaotic mixture of sound.

Mik: Create something from separate components (e.g. mik the dinner).

Mikkin A Wile Ship At: Not being very successful; pathetic effort.

Mikkin Fisses: Pulling facial contortions.

Mikkin Sheep's Eyes: Fluttering the eyelids to attract the opposite sex.

Mik Up: Get back on speaking terms with; face cosmetics used by women (and sometimes men).

Mimmy Gollagur: Mamie Gallagher.

Mind Yur Big Splas: Please move your feet.

Missin: Description of car not running smoothly.

Moderin: Contemporary; up to date.

Mulk: White liquid obtained from cows and taken as a nourishing drink.

Munce: Plural of month.

Narra Nan: Insult levelled at thin mean person.

Naw, Am A Liar: Hold on, I think I've made a mistake.

Naw, Am Haff Left: Quip in response to question "are you all right?"

Nawhin: Nothing.

Ned The Kwa: Term applied to person who displeases another.

Neet: Insect in scalp.

Nibbers: People who live in the same street or housing estate; a popular TV soap programme.

Nice Ti Yur Fis But Wud Stik A Knife In Yur Back: Treacherous; two faced.

Nick: Put out half-smoked cigarette; to steal.

Niver Dips A Han: Not over-enthusiastic about doing chores or spending money.

Nixt Time Wur Lukin Fur Hot Water We'll Send Fur Ye: Joking remark made to rejected blood donor.

None A May Notion: No intention of doing so.

No Sense: Prone to illogical action.

Not All There: Unbalanced; not fully in control.

Not A Mute: No sound; completely quiet.

Not A Nounce: Not very sensible; naive.

Not A Pik On Ye: Underfed; skinny.

Not Fussed On: Not too keen about.

No Toe: Nonsense nickname for friend.

Obcast: Bring up past misdeeds to embarass or compromise.

Oddyince: People in the auditorium; the listeners.

On The Batter: Up and about and working hard.

Open: Inflict injury on someone's head.

Optober: The tenth month of the year.

Orfant: Parentless child alone in the world.

Ornament: Derisory term for person of dull personality.

Orr Ite: Okay? How are you today?

Oul Blow: Person who embellishes story; windbag.

Oul Boot: Severely ugly person.

Oul Crack: Unacceptable talk or behaviour.

Oul Lilt A Da: Unwelcome character; bore.

Oul Sickener: Bore; distasteful character.

Oul Stickin Plaster: Hanger on; unwanted companion.

Pantamine: Yuletide stage extravaganza; a laughable situation.

Parly: Neutral zone in children's game of 'Tig'.

Patsy Quinn: French Derry City football star, Pascal Vaudequin.

Peeana: Large musical instrument with black and white keys.

Peeky: Pale looking; appearing unwell.

Peg: Throw.

Pihnt: Coloured liquid used for decorating walls etc.

Pillakiss: Cover for bed cushion.

Pinnicklty: Extremely fussy; annoyingly meticulous about detail.

Pist: Sticky gel-like substance used for hanging wallpaper.

Plank Yursel Down: Occupy a place where you're not entirely welcome.

Plits: Pieces of round porcelain for eating dinner off.

Poarn: Teeming with rain.

Plumpin: Raining heavily; boiling vigorously.

Pooch: Small leather money bag; gun holster.

Poor Wee Bit Ay A Wane: A young person who is being maltreated.

75

Poreshon: An amount or piece of (e.g. a poreshon of chips).

Pounded: Out of breath; exhausted.

Puck: Chosen; selected.

Puddy: Plaster-like substance for securing pane of glass in window frame.

Pull A lanker: Carry off a neat con trick; fool everybody.

Pullin An aulin: Treating roughly; manhandling.

Pull The Durr Behine Ye: Please close the door after you.

Punchur: Unwanted hole which causes tyre to deflate.

Purscripshun: Note from doctor permitting patient to obtain medicine or pills from chemist.

Put A an On: Make physical contact in order to cause bodily harm.

Put In Ageenst Ye: Speaking ill of someone to cause them trouble.

Put Ye Aff Yur Notion: Make you change your mind.

Put Ye In Minda: Make you think of; remind you of.

Randi Boo: Noisy gathering; mêlée.

Rasslin: Type of close-contact sport akin to judo.

Razure: Instrument for shaving hair off face and other parts of the body.

Real Derry: Having a pronounced Derry accent.

Real Dose: Insufferable person; pest.

Rickety Wheel: Circular spinning contraption used as a means of gambling at funfair.

Rickle A Bones: Thin frail person.

Riddly Gun: Automatic weapon.

Right Oul Screw: Substantial sum of money.

Rinnin: Precipitation.

Rise A Whole Stink: Create a serious fuss or disturbance.

Rissin: Running in competition against others; moving fast.

Roarin Outta Im: Shouting at the top of his voice.

Roulin: Moving along the ground in the manner of a wheel.

Rubbitch: Waste collected by the binman; stupid talk.

Ruinated: Completely spoiled or destroyed.

Ruin The Coops: Spoil everything for everybody.

Run Away Wi Yursel: Go off at a tangent; get confused.

Runnin About Lik A Yo-yo: In a tizzy; searching frantically.

Runnin Roun Lik Sumfin Not Wise: Mental condition giving cause for concern.

Runnin Ti The Doctors Wi Yur Ears: Badly in need of having your ears syringed or suffering from some other auditory problem.

Rushie: Frenetic form of street football for kids.

Say Black, Ye'll Niver Git That Back: Said by children at the conclusion of a successful business transaction.

Scaldie: Young, featherless bird.

Scalp: Sharp slap (usually administered to unruly child).

Scar: Shock or fright.

Schoolboard: Truancy officer.

Scoodle: Nip off in a hurry to do a little errand.

Scraggly: Very untidily dressed; unkempt.

Scratcher: Bed.

Scrillions: Very large number, precise value unknown.

Scrinkly: Describes the sound of tinfoil

Sendnil: Weekly Derry newspaper, freely on sale.

Settle Yur Head: Relax; take it easy.

Shadda: Dark image cast by person or object blocking off light.

Shake Hans, Bror, Yure A Rogue An Am A Norr: Friendly greeting from adult to child.

She Cud Liv Aff The Smell Ay An Oily Rag: She's a very thrifty lady.

She Hinks She Is Sumfin: She has big ideas about herself; a would-be snob.

She's More Pihnt On Er Than Wat's In Carlin's: She wears far too much make-up.

Shift: Type of nightshirt.

Shintalla: Large housing estate, north of Derry city centre.

Shooey Swinny: Hugh Sweeney.

Showlders Lik An Olive Oil Bockle: A bit on the thin side.

Show Up: Completely humiliate in public.

Shuman Beins: People; Homo sapiens.

Singil: One unit; unmarried person.

Sk'boo: Convenient alias when reluctant to give real name.

Skip It An Play Gulf: Never mind, forget it.

Skivin': Feigning illness or using excuse in order to avoid doing work; malingering.

Slup Up Yur Sloup There's More In The Slaucepan: A little nonsense to encourage children to eat.

Smoller: Suffocate by means of placing something over the mouth.

Snoodle: Sidle up craftily to someone with the intention of gaining their favours.

Sore Dose: Hard to stick; unlikeable person.

Soun Job: Satisfactory outcome for all concerned.

Spisser: One who is perpetually in a world of his own.

Spiss Kadett: One undergoing training to be a 'spisser'.

Spoil The Meetin: Throw a spanner in the works; interrupt current plans.

Square Up: Pay outstanding monies owed.

Stick: Stand or tolerate.

Still Shukin About: Getting around reasonably well.

Stittmint: Unwelcome letter from bank giving details of one's financial status.

Stoul: Taken without owner's consent.

Strainey: Small round object that tricksters try to pass off as genuine marble.

Strenth: Measure of one's physical capabilities.

Strik May Stiff Stone Dead: I'm definitely not telling lies.

Stychay: Likeness of person carved in stone.

Sumfin: Generic term for matter.

Sure Yur Da Wuz No Good, Yur Ma Wuz No Good, An All Baylongin Ti Ye Wuz No Good: I have doubts about your family's integrity.

Surra Mourne: Sarah Moran.

S'uss: Right, we're all set.

Swing ur: Be so enraged as to attempt violence.

Swundle: Blatantly cheat out of money or other possessions.

Symmetry: Place to bury the dead.

Tackle: Attempt to smooth talk a girl; query a past indiscretion.

Talk Ti May, Wud Ye: Female's request to friend when trying to hide from some unwelcome would-be suitor.

Tanted: Rotten (as of fruit).

Tatched: Connected to (e.g. the bike was tatched to the railings).

Tearin Wan Anoller: Violent altercation (usually between children).

Tear Lumps Aff: Give a severe dressing-down to.

Teem: Drain off excess water from boiling potatoes.

Tell Iz Sumfin We Don't Know: I know that.

Tendy Wan Faverit: The horse that's certain to win the race.

That Bitts Banagher And Banagher Bitt The Divil: A nine days' wonder that lasts for ten.

That Boy: Sneering reference to disliked male, regardless of age.

That'll Giv Ye Warts: Reprimand to child not to let air from balloon blow on to her/his face.

That Oul Brute: That uncouth male.

That's A Norr Hing: I'll tell you something else by the way.

That's Fur Me Ti Know And You Ti Fine Out: I know but I'm certainly not telling you.

That's Gran: I'm happy that we can agree.

That's In Front Ay Sumfin: Said when someone deviates from usual behaviour.

That's My Excuse, What's Yur's? You're just as bad as me.

That's Orr Ite Fur You: I don't care about you, what about me?

That's You Toul Aff: Sympathetic consolation after verbal rebuke.

That's Wile Nice A Ye: Thanks for nothing.

That Wud Fit Finn Ma Cool: I think your clothes are a bit too big for you.

That Wun Wud Go Thru Ye: Isn't it very cold today?

Thed: Fine cotton used for sewing.

The Nurls: Chickenpox,

The Oul Boy: My father.

The Reek Wudda Knocked Ye Down: There was an awful stench

There's More John Orrs Than Wan John Orr: There's more than one person with the same name.

The Shows: The pictures; the movies.

The Stitt: The Republic of Ireland.

The Wanderin Jew: Name for unsettled person.

Thick: Not intelligent.

Thon Donor: That stupid old so-and-so.

Thon's Hit: That's it.

79

Threble: Threefold; optimistic bet in turf accountant's entailing three horses.

Three Dee Orinje: Lemonade drink from Wee Johnny's shop formerly in Bishop St.

Throw The Head: Completely lose control; go berserk.

Throw Yursel Tigether: Get dressed in a hurry.

Thru Goin: Description of unmanageable child.

Thruppins: Three pence in old money.

Tibble: Square wooden piece of furniture with four legs.

Ti Hell Wi Obcastin: Some things are better left unsaid.

Tik A Fit: Recoil in shock at unwelcome news or event.

Tik Down: Defame someone's character; maliciously criticise.

Tikkin A Wile Han At: Making a fool of; joking with.

Tikkin In: Being admitted to hospital.

Tom The Divil Cudn't Scar Ye: Why don't you drop the pretence of being afraid?

Top: Little handle in sink for turning water off and on.

Touch: Accost for a loan of some money.

Touched: Slightly off balance mentally.

Toul: Told; imparted information to.

Toul Ti The Bone A Yur Nose: Told off straight to your face with no punches pulled.

Trailin: Setting out on an unrewarding errand.

Trowses: Long pants.

Twenny: Four short of two dozen.

Two Burnt Holes In A Blanket: Descriptive of eyes after a night of little sleep or heavy drinking.

Two Hairs Past A Freckle: I haven't a clue what time it is, I haven't got a watch.

Wa? I didn't hear you; say it again.

Wabblin Brush: Implement for applying shaving soap to the face.

Wait An Al Buy Ye A Dummy Tit: Don't be such a baby.

Wan Bitta Harm (Didn't Do May): Had no detrimental effect.

Wan Poun Wan: One guinea in predecimalisation days.

Wan Word From Me An He Does What He Liks: Admission by parent that he/she has little control over a child.

Want A Tista Salt? Hint to someone to stop biting their nails.

Wan Yeer Oul: One year old.

Warped Jute: Weirdo.

Wash Yur Mouth Out Wi Soap An Holy Watter: There's no need for all that profanity.

Watch The Material: Please keep your hands off my new suit.

Wat's Bitin Yur Cookie? What's the matter?

Wat Size De Ye Wear? Would you mind stamping out my cigarette butt?

Wat's The Damage? How much do I owe you?

Wat's Yur Beef? What is it you wish to complain about?

Watta Nunder God's That? Shocked reaction to loud noise or unusual sound.

Way A Goin On: General, everyday manner.

Wee Article: Cheeky, forward child.

Wee Bibby: Very young child.

Wee Birdie: Light kiss.

Wee Curt: Pleasant little cuddle with member of the opposite sex.

Wee Lick: Light dusting; quick wash.

Wee Low Set: Small in stature; diminutive.

Wee Mat'ney Coat: Little garment for the child.

Wee People: Children; young adults.

Wee Pitcher: Supporting film in cinema.

Wee Reek: Furtive smoke of cigarette.

Wee Wane Wi An Oul Woman's Head: Description of child too advanced for its years.

We Niver Died A Winter Yit: Cheer up! Things can only get worse.

Whaddyye Want – Blud? Do you not think you've taken enough from me?

Whaddyye Want Fur Nawhin? You're lucky you're getting what you're getting.

When Hunger Comes In The Durr, Pride Flies Out The Wunda: Poor people have to accept charity.

Where De Ye Burry Yur Dead? You're full of hot air.

Where's The Wun That Dried Yur Last Hippin? I don't know where he/she/it is.

Whole Mouthful: Barrage of profanity; a string of oaths.

Whole Tribe: A very large family.

Who's Yur Man? Who does he think he is?

Wile About: Madly in love with.

Wile Bad: Very ill.

Wile Big Connection: Large circle of family and friends.

Wile Curse: Terribly uncouth; very rough around the edges.

Wile Footery: Small and hard to work with; person who works in an irritating manner.

Wile Kis: Humorous, outgoing sort of person.

Wile Messer: Someone incapable of acting in a responsible and decisive manner.

Wile Ti Luk At: Unbearable performance of artist or football team.

Winna Han? May I be of assistance?

Wistin: Frittering away (e.g. wistin time).

Work A Wee Move: Pull off a coup.

Wudd: Material trees are made from.

Wud Ye Mind Where Yure Puttin Yur Big Size Tens: Mind your feet.

Wummanbitter: Cowardly male who only picks fights with the weaker sex.

Wumman's Pitcher: Film more suited to the ladies; tear-jerker.

Wur Ye Born In A Fiel Ur Wat? Shut that door.

Wush Ye Wur As Good At Sayin Yur Prayers: Said when someone disapproves of another's actions.

Wussle: High frequency sound emitted from mouth; referee's instrument for controlling game.

Wutniss: Person called by court to testify; one who is present at some event.

Wuz Ay Wearin Dark Glasses? Jibe by girl when friend has just announced that someone fancies her.

Ye Cudn't Run A Raffle A Pancakes: Your aptitude for organisation leaves a lot to be desired.

Ye Cudn't Work In A Fit: Toiling isn't one of your strong points.

Ye'd Bay Hard Up Fur A: I wouldn't fancy that at all.

Ye'd Bay Litt Fur Yur Own Funeril: Your tardiness is quite unacceptable.

Ye'd Hink A Bomb Hit This Pliss: Reference to untidy house.

Ye'd Hink All The Cats In Derry Wuz Chewin At Yur Hair: Insensitive remark passed to someone who has just had a new hair-do (especially a modern one).

Ye'd Hink Sumwan Hit Ye Up The Bake Wi A Bag A Flour: Why do you wear so much face powder?

Ye'd Hink The Dead Lice Wuz Fallin Aff Ye: God but you're a lazy good-for-nothing.

Yahoo: Rowdy but usually harmless character.

Ye Big Girl Ye: Don't be such a drip.

Ye Cudn't Bay Up Ti Ye: You're worth the watching.

Ye Cudn't Lik Ye If Ye Wur After Hivin Ye: You're the most hateful person I know.

Yisterey: The day before today.

Yock: Awkward person at work; anything old and dilapidated.

Yungfla: Common term applied to male regardless of age.

Yure A Good Turn But There's A Better Wan In Yur Eye: You're not at all funny.

Yure Dependin On A Broken Stik: Don't have too much faith.

Yure Good Crack At A Wake: You're not a bit funny.

Yure In Fur It: Warning to child there's a hiding in store from parents.

Yure Lik Haf-Hung McNutt: Straighten your collar and tie.

Yure Lukin At: This is what it will cost you.

Yure Mad So Ye Are: That was a stupid thing to do.

Yure Quare An Green: Don't try to kid me.

Yure Some Boy, Hi: Expression of disappointment when let down by friend.

Yure Sorely Wrought: Stop complaining, will you.

Yure Yur Da/Ma In The Sod: Observation that child behaves like parent.

Yur Head's Full A Sweedie Mice: You're completely out of touch with reality.

Yur Head's Lik A Busby: You're in need of a haircut.

Yur Own's No Miss: Usual retort when someone makes a remark about some part of another's anatomy.

Yur Socks Need Soled An Heeled: It's time you were changing your hosiery.

Yur Tube's Out: You haven't a hope.

Dolled Up

THE *wile* BIG DERRY PHRASEBOOK

...A WHOLE RAKE A' NEW WANS!

A-clantic: Large expanse of water between Ireland and the U.S.A.

A Cudda Bitt 'Im Wi' May Cap: Derogatory comment about cumbersome boxer.

Addig: Space in roof of house where lots of bric-a-brac is stored.

Afflete's Fut: Medical condition causing unpleasant symptoms in the feet.

Ah Don't See Yur Name On It: Sarcastic retort by someone who's just been accused of occupying someone else's seat.

Ah Hivn't Got Two Hippinys Ti' Rub Daygeller: I'm afraid I'm a bit low on ready cash.

Ah Luv May Moller 'N' Faller: I hold my parents in high esteem.

Ah Niver As Much As Washed May Fis The Day: I've done absolutely nothing today.

Ah Niver Did: Indignant denial that you haven't done anything untoward.

Ah Niver G'outta The Dour: I have a very uninteresting social life.

Ah Putt May Futt In The Bucket, An Rutted The Bucket About: Another dangerous Derry tonguetwister.

Ah Sid: I said.

Ah Suppose Al Hifty: I don't want to, but I haven't much choice.

Ahundurd: Five score.

Ah Wud'nt Mind A Lyin' Week Wi' That Boy: Declaration by girl that she fancies a certain young lad.

Ah Wud'nt See You Stuck: Offer to help out financially, or otherwise.

Ah Wudn't Tik Ye As A Gift: You're not my type at all.

Ah Wull Jist: I certainly will.

Ah Wush: I wish.

A Joke's A Joke But Git Yur Bum Off The Pilla: Do you not think you're carrying things a bit too far?

Alasayshun: Large hairy dog of German origin.

Al Bust Your Snotter: I'll punch you on the nose.

Al Crown Ye: I'll inflict serious injury on your head.

Al Dance On Your Tonsils: Threat to someone that they're about to be severely trounced.

Al Gie Ye Two Guesses An' The First Wan Diz'nt Count: You know exactly what I mean.

Al Git Sittin' Yit: My work never seems to end.

Al Give Ye A Week Ti' Stop That: Please don't stop, I'm excited.

Allagitter: Long fearsome reptile found in the swamps and rivers of America and Africa.

Al Lift Lumps Outta Ye: I can be very vicious if provoked.

All Worked Up: In a state of sexual excitement; very anxious.

Al Tell Ye Fur Why: These are my reasons.

Al Tell Ye Wan Thing, An Thats Not Two: What I'm about to say is the gospel truth.

Amblins: Emergency vehicle that transports the sick and injured to hospital.

Am Easy: It's all the same to me.

Am I Black Or What? Why do you keep ignoring me?

Am Nixt: It's my turn now.

Am Wile Dry: I'm very thirsty.

A Nairaplane: Large flying machine with wings.

Anniversity: Day of the year on which some important event is remembered, eg. marriage.

Anoller Shirt'll Do Ye: I'm afraid you're on the way out.

A Nounch: Small measurement of weight.

Any Word? What's the latest news?

Archieteks: People who draw up plans for houses and other types of buildings.

Assept: Receive thing or service offered; take on board.

Attackted: Assailed physically.

A Tatchy Kis: Small case for luggage etc.

Avinyee: Tree lined street or road (e.g. Beechwood Avinyee).

A Wee Bit Of Fluff: Cuddly, comely maiden.

A Wee Burl Roun' The Fluer: A little episode of dancing.

A Wee Wane In A Pram Hiz More Sense 'N' You: Why don't you grow up.

A Whole Tribe: An extremely large family.

Aw Now: We know what you're up to.

A Wush A Wuz Ye: Aren't you lucky? I wish I was in your shoes.

Aw You Hiv It/Aw Yur Mikkin' It: Your financial status is much better than you're letting on.

Ay Cud'nt Bliss Meself: He was in an advanced state of intoxication.

Aye, On May Ma's Nerves: Usual answer to question, 'Are you working?'

Ay Fell Ore A Straw An' A Hen Keeked 'Im: Quip by friend of supposedly mortally injured person when someone enquires as to how he got his injuries.

Baird: Hair growing on face and chin, usually on a man.

Bare Pelt: Completely naked; starkers.

Barra: Small one wheeled cart used by gardeners and building workers.

Beardy Nanna: Woman with superflous hair on her face; man who always seems to have stubble.

Big Trubbs: Serious difficulties.

Brisses: 'Y' shaped leather contraption for holding up trousers.

Broke Out: Uncharacteristically spent or parted with some money.

Browned Off Derryman: Humourous nickname for an Asian gentleman.

Bucklins: Company who run holiday camps.

Budder: Yellow fatty substance used to spread on bread.

Busty Buttons: Nickname for fat person.

Big Yank: Member of the American Forces, regardless of size.

Bitta Booty: Short session of knocking a football about.

Bitter As Gall: Has an extremely tart, vinegary taste.

Bitt It Down Yur Neck: Encouragement to drink when drinker is reluctant to do so.

Black Hole: Place where religous bigotry is rampant.

Bleenger: Extremely noisy passing of wind.

Blew Up Lik A Barrage Bloon: Having put on a few extra pounds.

Bloon: Thin colourful plastic bag that can be filled with air and hung up as decoration at parties etc.

Bo 'N Arra: Ancient weapon used in hunting and archery.

Boot Ugly: Of a slightly less than attractive appearance.

Carrigan: Light, casual woolen jacket.

Catchin Flies: Standing with your mouth open looking surprised.

Catlick: Non-Protestant.

Certint: Absolutely sure.

Chipper: Not as costly; less expensive.

Chissin It: On the hunt for a wife; engaged in courtship.

Clap: Cowpat; heap of cow dung.

Clove Fut: The trademark of the devil, allegedly appearing to poor unsuspecting humans from time to time.

Clows: Your everyday apparel.

Clows Paig: Little wooden (or plastic) object used for securing clothes onto clothes line.

Come Easy, Go Easy, God Sen' Sunday: Description of laid back, not easily ruffled type.

Complint: Objection, either verbal or written.

Conshume: Eat entirely.

Cooert: Place where legal disputes are settled by a judge, and sometimes a jury.

Cuckle: Having an impediment of eyesight.

Cuttelry: Knives, forks, spoons, etc.

Dale: Distribute cards out to card players.

Dead Soldier: Empty Guinness bottle, contents just been drunk.

Derry Journal: Gossip; person who knows everything.

Diddin Ah? Didn't I?

Diddly Dee: Light hearted reference to Irish music.

Diffrint: Not the same; unalike.

Dilly Pippers: The everyday newspapers.

Dinty: Small in stature; petite.

Dit: Time of the month.

Diz Yur Sister Tell Ye Everything? Smug retort when being teased about being a womaniser.

Dolled Up: Well dressed; a picture of sartorial elegance.

Don't Be Sarry, Jist Be Careful: I wouldn't do that again if I were you.

Don't Furgit Not Ti' Come Back: Friendly words of departure to visitors who are just leaving.

Don't Start Me: I'd advise you to shut up.

Do The Pliss Up: Redecorate the house.

Durdy: Not very clean, messy.

Dyin' Lukin': Physical condition giving cause for concern.

Eat: Violently take issue with.

Ellafint: Large animal found in India and Africa.

Exkip: Flee; get away from captivity.

Eyday: Six dozen and eight.

Eye Ye Away? (So's The Smell): Friendly words of departure.

Eye Ye Paralysed Ur Wat? Do your own work you lazy sod.

Eye Ye Practisin' Fur Santa Claus Ur Watt? I see you're cultivating a beard.

Eye Ye Whalin' Away? Are you still going strong?

Fair Midden: Dirty female.

Faller: Male parent.

Febuwurry: Second month of the year.

Fe Ye: For you.

Fine: Feel, experience (e.g. I didn't fine a thing.)

Fingery Friel: Clumsy, fidgety person.

Fishie: Establishment that sells fish and chips.

Flash The Ash: Hand round cigarettes.

Fordy: Three dozen and four.

Frens: People who can be relied on.

Frigfiss: Unpleasant name for disliked person.

Frill: Feeling of excitement.

Fulla Wun: Inclined to suffer from flatulence.

Furiver: Everlasting; eternal.

Furgit: Fail to remember.

Futrot: Disease brought on by waterboots letting in, so causing feet to look shrivelled and white.

Gack: Stupid, awkward-looking person.

Gang-gureen: Serious disease causing rotting of the limbs.

Gimme A Hot Connection: Have you a light?

G' In Indy Libber: Entering the last stages of pregnancy.

Git Aff Yur Mark: Be accepted by member of the opposite sex as a companion for the night.

Git A Grip On Yur Underwear: Please try and bring yourself under control.

Git A Man In: Employ someone to do household repairs or decorations.

Git A Shift: Be allocated a new house.

Git In There An' Say I Sent Ye: Term of self congratulation.

Git Scriped: Go away; you're not on.

Gitt: Entrance to field.

Gitta Lenna: Borrow for a short period of time.

Gittin' Hung: About to enter a state of wedded bliss.

Git The Bars Wi': Assume a position of girlfriend or boyfriend.

Giv That Man A Food Parcel: 'Award' offered to male who's just announced how gallant or brave he's been.

God's Gurse Ye: May the Lord bring bad luck on you.

Go An' Boil Yur Head: Disgusted refusal of a request; definitely not.

Go Home Yur Naked/Go Home Yur Mother Wants Ye: Friendly banter directed towards opponents.

G'on An' Git Haffa Ton A That Dirt Aff Ye: I think it's about time you had a wash.

G'On A That Wi' Ye: Be off with you; tell that to the marines.

G'On Giv'is A Wee Tist: May I have some please?

Good Man Yersel': Well done old chap.

Grab A Sit: Please take a chair.

Great Wi': On very friendly terms with.

Gripps: Sweet fruit of the vine used for making wine.

Gritt: Part of fire that holds the coal in place.

Grittin: Metal covered hole along end of footpath to allow water to drain away.

Grodda: Shrine containing statue of the Virgin.

Growing Like A Cows Tail: Getting smaller, growing downwards.

Gunga Din: Good humoured nickname for friend (nothing to do with eastern gentlemen).

He Cud Peel An Orange In Ay's Pocket: He's not renowned for his generosity.

He'd Git Drunk On The Smell Of A Barman's Iprin/Suckin Brandyballs: His capacity for holding drink is suspect.

Heevy: Helping hand up over a fence or other obstacle.

He Wud'nt Give Ye The Itch If Ay Had Two Doses Of It: He's not a very generous person.

Hi, Git The Hair Outta Your Eyes: Unkindly remark to bald headed footballer when he misses the ball.

Hiv On: Play a joke on; playfully deceive.

Hivva Bitta Sense, Wull Ye: Patronising plea to antagonist (usually the worse for drink) who's determined to have a good fight.

Hiv Ye A Big Stik There? Request from agitated mother to friend when child misbehaves, hoping that child will take it as a threat.

Hog Nail Boots: Heavy leather footwear.

Houl Yur Tongue: I agree totally; it goes without saying.

How'd Ye Lik A Fat Lip? I'm getting very annoyed at you.

How's The Man? Greeting, usually by citizens on the periphery of city, Drumahoe, Tullyally etc.

92

I Could Laugh At You: You're behaviour shows a degree of inconsistency; why don't you practise what you preach.

If Ye Had An Air Ti' That Ye Could Sing It: Would you please stop going on about the same thing.

I'll Spit In Your Eye: I detest you.

Immeejitly: At once; right away.

In A Wile Stitt: Very distressed; in a terrible mess.

In Bad Twust: Not in a good mood; depressed.

In Bunch: Sharing the spoils equally.

Indeed 'N' Sowl Ah Wull Not: No way, Jose.

In Wi' A Shout: Having a reasonable chance of success.

Iprin: Light garment worn to protect clothes when washing dishes etc.

Iss: Highest card in suit.

Is Thur Anything Else Ye'd Lik' Ti' Know? Why don't ye mind your own business!

Is Thur Wan At Ye? Why are you scratching so much?

It's A Fit Day Fur Nether Man Nur Biste: That's the weather for staying indoors.

It's A Good Dose A Epsom's Ye Want: Would you stop complaining about your health.

It's All In The Way Ye Houl Yur Mouth: Easy isn't it?

It's Comin' Up On The Nixt Boat: There's nothing for you.

It's Dryin Up Fur Snow: Warning that inclement weather is on the way.

It's Dyed Aff 'Er Head: I suspect that that's not her hairs' natural colour.

It's Lik Tryin' Ti' Fine Holy Watter In An Orange Lodge: Extremely hard to come by.

It Wuz Liftin' Lumps Outta The Road: The precipitation was intense.

I Wuz In Wi' May Leg: Reason for a spell in hospital.

I Wuzn't Rared On That Ye Know: Indignant retort by someone who's just been reminded that they've neglected to pay a paltry sum of money owed.

Iz That Hard Ti' Sing? It's Damned Hard To Lissin Ti: You aren't exactly Pavarotti are you?

Iz Yur Arm Broke Ur Wat? I think it's your round.

Januwurry: First month of the year.

Jeer: Unmentionable part of the human anatomy not too far from the tail bone.

Jesus Wept: Exclamation of exasperation.

Jist Wanna Thim: Only one.

Joe Soap (Who Do You Think I Am)? Fictitious alias; do you take me for a fool?

Jook The Beetle: Name for crafty person.

Jurkin: Short light jacket with zipper at front.

Knyam: Cry, bemoan or complain unduly.

Kanna? May I?

Keekin' An' Flingin': Lashing out wildly with arms and legs.

Kine A Haff Middlin: Just average, mediocre.

Kinnlin: The basic essentials for making a fire (e.g. sticks, paper etc.)

Kipp: Piece of clothing resembling a cloak; piece of land jutting out into sea (e.g. Kipp of Good Hope).

Kipper: Trick or practical joke.

Kissin' The Altar Rails: What person perceived to be a hypocrite does every Sunday, while sinning the rest of the week.

Kittlin: Young pussy cat.

Knuspipper: Organ of the media.

Ladies And Gentlemen And Baldy Headed Countrymen: Shakesperian parody designed to attract the attention of anyone who'll listen.

Land In: Arrive on an unexpected visit, one which is perhaps not one hundred per cent appreciated.

Lave: Depart; go away.

Laverty/Lav: Place to do ones ablutions.

Lay Ar Faller: The Lord's Prayer.

Lay Go: Release me; unhand me at once.

94

Leller In Ti': Attack with vigour and gusto.

Lessa Yur Oul Buck: Don't be so cheeky now.

Let A Roar At: Shout at in an attempt to modify someones behaviour.

Libberarchie: American singer and pianist.

Libber Pardy: British political party.

Libery: Place where you go to borrow books and study.

Lik' A Dog's Hine Leg: In a very untidy and disordered condition.

Lik A Duntin' Bull: In a foul, bad tempered frame of mind.

Lik A Fibre Mattress: Unkind description of person with coarse and unkempt red hair.

Lik An Oul Woman Wi' A Straw Ass: Unable to take any rough treatment; description of very fragile individual.

Lik' A Week's Work: Difficult, arduous task.

Lik Two Matches Stickin' Out Ay A Spud: Unkind description of a small fat person with thin legs.

Lisses: Long pieces of string used for securing boots and shoes.

Lissin Mit: Ominous opener to further verbal, or possibly physical conflict.

Little Amuses The Innocent: Remark passed to someone who is caught playing with childish things.

Lost: Being in a position where talents aren't recognized or appreciated.

Lucky Duck: Childrens' description of recipient of good fortune.

Luk, I Cudn't Give Two Tuppeny Damns: I just couldn't care less.

Lukin' At The Style: Occupation, usually of the ladies, whereby they observe carefully what all the other girls are wearing.

Luks Lik Ye Wur Dragged Through A Hage Backroads: Of an unkempt, bedraggled appearance.

Luks Odd: Seems so different; completely changed.

Luk, There's Wee Johnny Laughin' At Ye: Attempt to embarrass crying child in order to get it to shut up.

Maisles: Contagious disorder where red spots appear on the body.

Man: Prefix or suffix to sentence.

'Member? Do you recall?

Midger: Determine by measuring tape or other means the dimensions of.

Midget: Minute insect whose bite causes great distress and irritation.

Mik A Mouth A Yersel: Disgrace yourself in public; act like an idiot.

Minellium: A thousand years
Moller: Female parent.

Moller A Sarras: Person who appears to carry all the troubles of the world on their shoulders.

Monkey Glands: Insult levelled at hateful type.

Mouthwash: Description of someone who bathes another in saliva while kissing.

Mussly: Of a strong, well developed appearance.

Naaaaa: Semi-negative answer when person is not sure if they mean yes or no.

Nags: Mens personal garments.

Nawhin Strange? No earth shattering news?

Nether Air Nur Smell: Devoid of musical form; tuneless.

Niver Diz A Tap: Is quite averse to anything resembling work.

Nixt Door Nibber: The person living closest to you.

Nose Lik A Bullhook: Unkind description of someone with a large curved proboscis.

Nuggit: Type of white soft toffee.

Nur Me Eller: You can count me out as well.

Oblege: Help out of difficulties; grant request.

Och Nawhin: Never mind; forget about it.

Octaypuss: Large sea creature with eight tentacles.

Oddamadig: Needing minimum supervision.(e.g. oddamadig washing machine).

Oddim: The season preceding winter.

On Ti' A Good Thing: Discovering a lucrative line of business (usually by chance).

Ord'nray: Run of the mill; mundane.

Oul Hardie Hole: Nickname for stingy person.

Oul Heiffer: Insulting name for female.

Oul Poser: Person who prances around provocatively, trying to pretend that it's their natural deportment.

Oul Relic: Unwelcome, boring type of person.

Oul Slippy Tit: One who gets away with 'murder'; jammy individual.

Oul Wormy: Most unpleasant name for weak, disliked person.

Paddles: Foot rests on bicycle used as means of propulsion.

Pamp: Sound car horn.

Pass No Remark: Ignore; don't take any notice.

Pee The Bed: Dandelion.

Pickin' An' Dabbin: Not exactly eating meals voraciously.

Pick The Bones Outta That: Said by someone who's just spat on the ground.

Pignose: Unkindly reference to part of another's anatomy.

Piss: Rate or velocity.

Pistrey: Assorted sweet buns.

Pitchur A Misery: Of a somewhat crestfallen appearance.

Plank: Hide or stash away for later.

Plett: Long tail of interwoven hair on head.

Plowter: Plod through mud; trudge along.

Polar Neck: Type of jumper that goes right up to the chin.

Probbly: In all likelihood.

Propergander: Lies put out by governments in times of conflict or war.

Pull On Ye: Get dressed in a hurry.

Pulled Up: Confronted by a demand to explain past indiscretions.

Punchy: Dense; not in command of ones senses.

Punkawalla: Affectionate nickname for friend.

Put The Wunda In: Break the window.

Put Yur Han' Ti' That Dour: Please close the door.

Quare Form: In good spirits; happy.

Queeng: Female monarch.

Quzz: Event where chairperson asks questions on various subjects and panel or audience answer.

Qwud: One pound sterling.

Raycord: Circular wax or vinyl recording of music or speech.

Ready Fur The Ragbag: Description of clothes (usually still worn) that have seen better days.

Ready To Squeal: Unable to take anymore.

Ressliss: Fidgety; unable to relax.

Rift: Bring up gas from stomach.

Right Oul Half: Attractive female.

Rubber Dinky: Small inflatable boat.

Run In Ti': Meet up with; encounter.

Sail In: Appear suddenly, usually uninvited.

Sanitry Man: Person who periodically calls to make sure your lavatory is clean.

Say Boo: Some Derry singer's interpretation of line in Jim Reeves song 'Anna Marie' (C'est vous).

Scandal: Gossip; news.

See If You Brak Yur Leg, Al Brak Yur Oller Wan: Sadistic warning given by concerned parent to child who persists in indulging in playful but dangerous activities.

Seezy: It's easy.

Sellatipp: Sticky tape used for securing parcels etc.

Serpent: Devious, untrustworthy type.

Set Fut In: Visit someplace after a long absence.

Ship: Type of unsliced loaf.

Shipway Pliss: Pedestrianised area in front of Guildhall.

Shugger: Crystals of either cane or beet used for sweetening tea or in the making of confectionery.

Shut Yur Big Yappin' Mouth, Wud Ye: For God's sake give it a rest.

Siff: Secure from harm; hole in wall for storing money and other valuables.

Siff's A Row A Houses In Fahan Street: Extremely unsafe; about to fall.

Siller: Sea going member of the armed forces.

Sint: Deceased person who has been canonized by the church; goody type.

Sittin' Wittin': Hanging about in an impatient and irritated frame of mind.

Six Months: What you get when you feel you're talking to yourself.

Skittery: Small in size or number.

Skitts: Equipment that can be attached to the feet for purposes of either sport or recreation, and can either be 'ice' or 'roller'.

Skive Off: Sneak away without doing fair share of the chores.

Slingy: Primitive weapon made from 'Y' shaped branch and length of rubber and used to propel missiles through the air.

Slip Off, Nobody's Lukin': Advice given by fans to footballer who's not having a very good game.

Slit: Rectangular tile used in roofing houses etc.

Soun' Filla: Good decent upstanding sort of chap.

Sowl Out: Nothing left to sell.

Spastic: Cruel name for person not liked. No relation to the physically handicapped.

Stacks A People: A very big crowd.

Stan' At Peace, Wull Ye: Will you please stop moving about.

Stanin' Gawkin': Staring with mouth open and blank look on face.

Stews, Farts And Onions: Answer given by parent to child in reply to, 'What's for dinner?'

Stick On Ye: Get dressed hurriedly.

Stibble: Building where horses are fed and sheltered.

Stikkit: Acrimonious grunt when refused share of something.

Stinkin' Wi' Hunger An' Fartin' Wi' Pride: Reluctant to admit that you're poor.

Stumor: Person whose strongest trait is his stupidity.

Swalla: Swift flying birds who's appearance is reputed to herald the beginning of summer.

Tanked Up: Highly intoxicated and in a very volatile frame of mind.

Tartar: Unattractive name for rough, argumentative female; malevolent woman.

Tarts: Various types of pastry.

Taybrak: Short sojourn from work for some refreshment.

That's Anoller Sharp Wan: Is there no end to this cold weather?

That's My Story An' Am Stikin Ti' It: Weak excuse put forward by person when it's obvious to everyone that he's lying.

That's The First Signs: Medical diagnosis hinting at insanity given to someone overheard muttering to themselves.

The Crows Wur Puttin' Out Thur Tongues Wi' Heat: The temperature was abnormally high.

The Divil's Lukin' Outta Yur Eyes: Said by parent to child in an attempt to scare it into changing its naughty ways.

Them Bokeys'll Mik A Rope An' Drag Ye Down In Ti' The Quay: Dire warning from parent to child of what will befall them if they refuse to have their hair fine combed.

Them Oul Derry Wans: Light hearted reference by 'outsiders' to inhabitants of the Maiden City.

There's Nawhin' Ti' Ail Ye: You're quite capable of doing it yourself.

The Saftest Thing About That Boy Is His Teeth: He's not as soft as he lets on.

The Snotters Wuz Trippin' Him: His nose needed cleaning.

The Stitts: America.

The Th'ee Stoogies: Forties/fifties American comedy trio.

The Tune The Oul Cow Died Wi': Sound emanating from 'singers' bereft of melody and tone.

The Voice In The Wulderness: Sound of person speaking up in a futile attempt to draw attention to problem.

Things Are Lukin' Black In The Coalmine: Jovial term saying that all isn't well.

Thote: Cylindrical part of body between head and trunk which facilitates the passage of food and air.

Thurday: Two and a half dozen.

Thur Neck's Broken: Description of extremely spoiled children.

Thur's More Hair On A Billiard Ball: Unkind remark passed to male who is slightly thin on top.

Tikkit Thick: Respond unfavourably to joke or prank.

Tik Up: About to change for the better (e.g. I think the weather's about to 'tik up').

Tik The Good Outta: Perform a generous act then negate it by doing something mean.

Tipp Acordur: Electronic device for recording sound.

Tizz: It is.

Tizzn't: It isn't.

Tongue Hingin' Out: Dying of thirst; green with envy.

Too Sweet To Be Wholesome: Means that someone is not as nice as they would have you believe.

Toothick: Intense pain in the nerves of the mouth, instigating an unwelcome visit to the dentist.

Triller: Small cart affair towed behind vehicle; short preview of film.

Turn: Be converted to another religion.

Turn On Yur Heel: Abruptly leave and bring conversation to an end.

Two On Ti' Wan Kills A Man: Uneven contest.

Twust: Bend out of shape; early sixties dance.

Twyste: Two times.

Ukalily: Small guitar shaped musical instrument with four strings.

Up My Back Fur A Hump: I don't know where it is and I don't care.

Up The Country: Anywhere in Ireland outside Derry.

Up The Wudden Hill: Where children go to get to bed.

Unknownst Ti' May: Without my knowledge or consent.

Vennel: Pipe for water to drain away.

Vile-o: One who was completely forgotten when good looks and other attractive attributes were handed out.

Viper: Backbiter; one whose veracity is suspect.

Voice Lik A Foghorn: Not exactly dulcet toned; of a gruff vocal nature.

Wadder: Clear liquid used for drinking and washing; H^2O.

Wagon: Derogatory term from yesteryear descriptive of female with less than attractive features.

Wan A Yese: One at a time please.

Warewulf: Mythical creature who allegedly could change from a man into a horrible lupine monster.

Watch Ye Don't Loss Yur Finger: Would you please stop picking your nose.

Wat Possessed Ye? Why did you act the way you did?

Wat's That, A Scotch Mist? Rebuke by someone who asks another to find something without success then finds it himself.

We All Hiv Wur Wee Ways A Goin' Mad: Sarcastic answer by someone who has just had one of their little eccentric foibles pointed out.

Wee Feel: A little romantic messing around.

Wee Hitler: Small upstart who has a modicum of power over the general public (e.g. Traffic Warden).

Wee Nadger: Term for youngest or smallest in the family.

Wee Rub: Light embrocation designed to alleviate chest congestion and other unpleasant aches and pains associated with bad weather (e.g. Vick).

Wee Scrip: A quick shave.

Wee Stout Man/Woman: Short, plump person.

Weird 'N' Wonderful: Out of the ordinary; unusual.

Well'tin St: Area of Bogside no longer in existence.

Well Turned Out: Neatly presented; smartly dressed.

Whaddy Ye Doin' This Weller? Have you found employment?

Whats Bitin Your Cookie? What's the matter?

When Ye Put On Your Shoes In The Mornin' Ye Niver Know Who'll Tik' Em Off: You can't be sure when you're going to die.

Whinging: Insistent quiet crying or moaning.

Who Eye Ye On Fur? Who do you support?

Who Owns Ye Yo Ho? Expression of disbelief.

Why Don't Ye Bring Yur Bed Wi' Ye? Advice to person who's caught laying down on the job.

Why Don't Ye Put It In A Glass Kis An Throw Sugar At It: Facetious advice given to someone who is over protective about one of their possessions.

Widder: Person in restaurant who serves up the meals.

Wig: Pull someones hair.

Wicked/Woeful: Awful; terrible (as of performance).

Wile Bouncy: Very springy (as of bed).

Wile Clatter A Wanes: A family many in number and young in years.

Wile Fur: Has a strong inclination to.

Wile Keekin': Serious beating up.

Wile Neck: Having no sense of embarrassment or shame.

Wile Pisty Lukin': Of a pale, wan appearance.

Wile Slippy: Very slippery.

Wile Stuck: In need of immediate cash or other commodity.

Wile Wist: Pointless squandering of resources.

Wile Witt: Extremely heavy.

Wile Wundy Weller: Extremely unsettled climatic conditions.

Wistcoat: Short, tight, sleeveless jacket.

Work A Lyin' Week: Toil for seven days in lieu of wages.

Wrong Sort: Not of the proper religious persuasion.

Wud Ye Lik' May Ti' Dance Ye A Jig? Who do you think you're trying to boss about?

Wud Ye Tik That Hump Off Yur Back: Would you please stop slouching.

Wud Ye Tik That Oul Fis Aff Ye: For God's sake cheer up.

Wull: Fleece of sheep used for knitting jumpers etc.

Wullered: Dried up and drooping.

Wully Winkle: Santa Claus's sidekick who, for a few weeks before Xmas, checks to see that children are in bed at a reasonable hour; seasonal Peeping Tom.

Wun: Fast moving air.

Wunbush: Little shrub that grows in fields and along hedgerows.

Wunter: The coldest season of the year.

Wupp: Long leather implement used for encouraging horses to run faster, or for flogging people.

Wur Qwuts: We are now on equal terms.

Wursels: Us; we people.

Wur Ye In The Bookies? Question designed to draw attention to the fact that ladie's slip is showing.

Wuspur: Quiet word in ear.

Wuttlin: Carving little shapes out of wood (usually with a penknife).

Wur Ye Out Wunda Cleanin'? Oh ho, you've got a ladder in your stocking.

Wur Ill Ley? I wonder where they've got to?

Wuth: Accompanying (i.e. The dog was wuth the man).

Ye Can Stan' There Ti' Yur Googy Wuthers: There's not much point in you hanging round here.

Ye Cudn't Beat
(1) Snow Ay A Rope:
(2) Casey's Drum:
Sneering retort to someone who threatens violence.

Ye Cudn't Box Eggs: You aren't exactly Mohammed Ali.

Ye Cudn't Keek A Hen Ti' Death: You're not a very good footballer, are you?

Ye Cudn't Pass Yur Watter: What a terrible footballer you are.

Ye Cudn't Throw Up: Severe criticism of imcompetent darts thrower.

Ye Cud See A Flay Walkin' Up Yur Leg: Observation that persons trousers are a bit on the tight side.

Ye Dirty Dog Ye: Light hearted reprimand when someones played a joke on someone else.

Ye Don't Want Much De Ye? Do you not think you've set your sights a bit high?

Ye Don't Hiv A Good Word Ti' Say 'Bout Nobody: I suppose you're whiter than white.

Ye Do Right: Words of encouragement to person in the act of being less than helpful to another.

Ye'd Think Ye Niver Washed Fur A Week: Your personal hygiene leaves a lot to be desired.

Ye'd Think Ye Wur Vaccinated Wi' A Gramophone Needle: Would you please stop talking for a moment.

Ye Know I Don't Allow Ye Ti' Do That: Plea by embarrassed mother to wayward child who repeatedly does something in public that he's not supposed to.

Yella: Bright pastel colour; cowardly.

Ye'll Bay Bringin' Them Out Lit Nixt: Jibe directed at miser who has just secretly ignited a cigarette without offering any to others.

Ye'll Bay Pickin' Leller Outta Yur Ass Fur A Week: I'm about to administer you a hefty kick.

Ye'll Be All Right In The Mornin' Sure: Why are you acting so strange?

Ye'll Hiv A Long Witt: I wouldn't hold my breath if I were you.

Ye'll Niver Hiv Luck: Bemoaning what was considered the dubious good fortune of another.

Ye'll Not Die: Unsympathetic response to person who complains of a minor injury or illness.

Ye May Mik Do: I'm afraid you'll have to make the best of what you've got.

Ye Must Bay Hard Up Fur A Bite: You'd eat anything, wouldn't you?

Ye Nearly Had A Fry: Hard luck old chap.

Ye Niver Go Nowhere: Admonishment to person who fails to fulfill his Christian duties.

Ye Niver Toul May That Bar: Why did you fail to divulge that important piece of information?

Ye Tuk That Outta May This Day: Words of rebuke to child by swearing parent.

Ye've A Brass Neck On Ye/Ye've a neck lik Nelson: You've got a nerve.

Ye've Neller Manners Nur Breedin': You're as common as muck.

Ye've No Blud In Ye: Why are you always complaining of the cold?

Ye've No Ern: You haven't a hope in hell.

Ye've Some Hope: You've absolutely no chance.

Ye Wudn't Git Peace Ti' Do Nawhin: Is there no end to these interuptions?

You Give Me The Pip: You annoy me.

You'll Eat Hit B'fore Hit Eats You: Admonishment to child who sulks and won't eat.

You're A Good 'Un But You'll Go: Patronising remark.

You Wurn't Behine The Dour When They Wur Given Out Eller, Wur Ye? Angry retort by someone who has just had some part of their anatomy commented on.

Yur A Wile Bad Wunda: Would you please stop obstructing my view.

Yur Bums Out The Wunda: You're wrong; you've had it.

Yur Easy Annoyed: Don't be so touchy.

Yur Not G'nout Lik That Eye Ye? Do you not think you could dress a little better on social occasions? (Usually directed at husband from wife).

Yur Talkin' Thru' Yur Hat: You're talking complete nonsense.

Yur Wile So Ye Are: Oh you're absolutely awful.

The Great Derry Quiz

Do you have the qualities to be a fully fledged citizen of Derry? Answer the questions below and find out.

MEN

(Tick one box)

1. Can you eat at least half a dozen baps? **Yes ❑ No ❑**

2. Can you push a pram with one hand, with your free hand in your back pocket, trying to look as if you don't do it all the time? **Yes ❑ No ❑**

3. Can you smoke a quarter inch butt without burning your fingers?
Yes ❑ No ❑

4. Are you a pub quiz addict and spend a fair portion of your spare time memorising all the capital cities of the world? **Yes ❑ No ❑**

5. Do you spend at least six hours a week in the bookies or a card school?
Yes ❑ No ❑

6. Have you ever received an invitation to the Bru's annual dance?
Yes ❑ No ❑

7. Have you ever been photographed for the Derry Journal with either Bishop Daly or Dr. Tom McGinley? **Yes ❑ No ❑**

8. Have you ever had a request played on Radio Foyle for 'anyone that knows me'? **Yes ❑ No ❑**

9. Do you use the words 'mucker' or 'yes hi' regularly? **Yes ❑ No ❑**

10. Are you in the Cursillo movement and walk to Knock every year? (this also applies to females) **Yes ❑ No ❑**

11. Have you ever owned, or even walked, a greyhound? **Yes ❑ No ❑**

12. Have you ever gathered brock or sold sticks? **Yes ❑ No ❑**

13. When asked to sing in a pub, do you render either 'Starry Night', The Candy Store' or, even worse, both? **Yes ❑ No ❑**

14. Do you wear white socks and black 'slip ons', and if over thirty are you always five years behind the latest fashions? **Yes ❑ No ❑**

15. Have you ever gone to England for a fortnight and returned with an English accent? **Yes ❑ No ❑**

16. Can you dance the 'Corinthian Crawl' or have you tried to jive to 'rave' music?
Yes ❑ No ❑

17. Have you ever 'scranned' from your dole cheque? **Yes ❑ No ❑**

18. Do you prefer to watch Derry City from the College Field or the graveyard rather than the Brandywell Stadium itself? **Yes ❑ No ❑**

19. Do you understand the book 'Talk of the Town'? (also applies to females)
Yes ❑ No ❑

20. Are you still convinced that the showbands are about to make a comeback?
Yes ❑ No ❑

21. Do you own a Derryman's Diary? **Yes ❑ No ❑**

WEEMIN

1. Can you run with your arms folded, with absolutely no movement of the chest? **Yes ❑ No ❑**

2. Can you sit crosslegged, tucking the toes of the upper leg behind the calf of the lower leg? **Yes ❑ No ❑**

3. Do you actively seek out the latest scandal or bars? **Yes ❑ No ❑**

4. Do you wear your curlers and house slippers to bingo? **Yes ❑ No ❑**

5. Do you like apple turnovers or a 'lodger'? **Yes ❑ No ❑**

6. After a domestic dispute have you admonished you husband, or boyfriend, with the words 'You'll niver lift yur han' ti' me again as long as ye liv' or 'I'm tikkin' these wanes up ti' me ma's'? **Yes ❑ No ❑**

7. Do you prefer to live at most two doors from your mother?
Yes ❑ No ❑

8. Have you ever worked in a shirt factory and occasionally slunk off in the afternoon to go to the matinee with your bars? **Yes ❑ No ❑**

9. Do you have a female child named either Aisling or Edel? **Yes ❑ No ❑**

10. Can you exhale a cloud of cigarette smoke and at the same time make a loud crack with a chewing gum bubble? **Yes ❑ No ❑**

11. Have you ever referred to a would be suitor as 'a tube'? **Yes ❑ No ❑**

12. When invited to sing in a pub or at a party, is your repertoire limited to 'One Day At A Time' or 'Baby Blue'? **Yes ❑ No ❑**

13. Can you jive with one hand while holding your skirt down with the other and simultaneously smoking a fag? **Yes ❑ No ❑**

14. Are you at least two months behind on your Credit Union book? **Yes ❑ No ❑**

15. Is the highlight of your week a Sunday night in St Eugene's parish hall with your wee carry out? **Yes ❑ No ❑**

16. Are you an avid listener of Sean 'not too far from Radio Foyle' Coyle's City Factory Show? **Yes ❑ No ❑**

17. Have you at least one relation who works in the same factory? **Yes ❑ No ❑**

18. Do you still hanker for the days the when the yanks were here? **Yes ❑ No ❑**

19. Do you know the words of 'The Town I Loved So Well' off by heart? (applies to males also) **Yes ❑ No ❑**

20. Do you allow a man to put his hands inside your coat in cold weather when courting? **Yes ❑ No ❑**

21. Have you ever bought someone a Derryman's Diary? **Yes ❑ No ❑**

How did you score?

Twenty one – Congratulations. You're a perfect specimen of Derryhood. Award yourself a certificate.

Fifteen to twenty – You're highly commended and definitely in with a shout.

Ten to fourteen – Well done, but try a little harder and you'll make it.

Six to nine – I'm afraid you'll have to pull your (white) socks up if you want to be a serious contender.

Three to five – The chances of you ever achieving full Derry status, unfortunately, are slim indeed.

Less than three – No way Jose! Forget it and try a lesser place like Limavady.

Guildhall

AM WILE SMART SO A AM

University

BY VIRTUE OF THE POWER VESTED IN IT BY THE
CHARTER AND STATUTES AND BY THE AUTHORITY
OF THE SENATE, THE UNIVERSITY HAS THIS DAY
CONFERRED THE DEGREE OF

TRUE DERRYHOOD

....

ON

....

HAVING COMPLETED A COURSE IN THE STUDY OF
DERRYISMS, INCLUDING AN INTENSIVE STUDY OF THE WILE
BIG DERRY PHRASEBOOK AND SUCCESSFUL COMPLETION OF
THE FINAL EXAMINATION

Signed on behalf
of the University   *Seamus Mc Connell*
....

Seamus McConnell
Honorary Chancellor

Other titles available from
GUILDHALL PRESS

DESIGN
–POSTERS, FLYERS, LOGOS, STATIONERY
INTERNET
– SITE DESIGN & PUBLISHING
PUBLISHING SERVICES
– TYPESETTING, EDITING, PROOFING, CONTRACT PUBLISHING
PHOTO MANIPULATION
– GM PHOTOS, ALTERED, MODIFIED, DISTORTED

For further details see our websites at
www.ghpress.freeserve.co.uk
www.derry2000.freeserve.co.uk
www.quarecraic.freeserve.co.uk